Diabetic Desserts

Betty Wedman, Ph.D., R.D.

CONTEMPORARY BOOKS
A TRIBUNE NEW MEDIA/EDUCATION COMPANY

Library of Congress Cataloging-in-Publication Data

Wedman, Betty.
    Diabetic desserts / Betty Wedman.
       p.   cm.
    Includes index.
    ISBN 0-8092-3388-6
    1. Diabetes—Diet therapy—Recipes.   I. Title.
RC662.W363   1996
641.5′6314—dc20   95-26393
                                 CIP

The American Diabetes Association and the American Dietetic Association have recently developed a series of nutritional education resources for people with diabetes including a revised edition of the *Exchange Lists for Meal Planning*. This project was overseen by a Steering Committee made up of members of the American Diabetes Association and the American Dietetic Association. Members of the Steering Committee included Madelyn Wheeler, MS, RD, CDE, Chair; Brenda Broussard, RD; Anne S. Daly, MS, RD, CDE; Joyce Green Pastors, MS, RD, CDE; Harold J. Holler, RD, CDE; Lea Ann Holzmeister, RD, CDE; and Hope S. Warshaw, MS, RD, CDE.

The writing committee for the revised edition of *Exchange Lists for Meal Planning* consisted of the following members: Harold J. Holler, RD, CDE, Chair; Phyllis Barrier, MS, RD, CDE; Nancy Cronmiller, MMSc, RD, CDE; Linda Delahanty, MS, RD; Marion Franz, MS, RD, CDE; and Madelyn Wheeler, MS, RD, CDE.

Featured on the cover: Fruit Tart, Killer Chocolate Cake, and Cookies and Cream Cheesecake (pages 70, 52, and 30)

Cover design by Kim Bartko
Cover photo by Chris Cassidy
Interior design by Terry Stone

Published by Contemporary Books, Inc.
Two Prudential Plaza, Chicago, Illinois 60601-6790
Manufactured in the United States of America
International Standard Book Number: 0-8092-3388-6
10   9   8   7   6   5   4   3   2   1

To all those individuals with diabetes
who thought I was unscientific when
I told them to use sugar instead of
sugar substitutes in their recipes

Contents

Preface *vii*

Acknowledgments *ix*

1 Introduction *1*

2 Cookies *5*

3 Bar Cookies *17*

4 Cakes *27*

5 Pies and Pastries *57*

6 Muffins and Quick Breads *73*

7 Holiday Favorites *81*

8 Other Favorites *103*

9 Dessert Beverages *121*

Appendix: Exchange Lists for
Meal Planning *129*

Index *145*

Preface

*S*top feeling guilty and deprived! Here is a way to enjoy your favorite desserts and still stay within your diabetes meal plan.

Two key things must be kept in mind when using these recipes:

- Limit portion sizes
- Limit frequency of use

Depending on your blood glucose management, you can enjoy these favorite foods by substituting them for other carbohydrates in your meal plan. Now you can indulge in chocolate chip cookies by skipping that baked potato at dinner. Or enjoy a brownie with your lunch by omitting a slice of bread on your sandwich. And you can add new variety to your breakfast by starting the day with a square of Sour Cream Coffeecake or a Gingerbread Muffin.

Cheating on your diabetic diet need no longer be a factor in your life. Enjoy, enjoy, enjoy. . . .

Acknowledgments

Many thanks to my loyal friends who served as tasters for these recipes. A special thanks to Bill Owens and Coralee Hayes who tasted almost every one of these recipes—and the failures—while providing helpful criticism for recipe modification.

Susan Busekrus and the staff at The Office Annex did a wonderful job typing and assembling the cookbook without the joy of tasting the recipes they labored over.

The recipe analysis was done using Computrition, Inc. software, courtesy of the Dietary Staff at Columbia Regional Medical Center at Bayonet Point, Hudson, Florida.

The food exchange lists in the Appendix are produced by the American Diabetes Association and the American Dietetic Association. The lists are based on the most current nutrient data available.

1

Introduction

The new nutrition guidelines for people with diabetes focus on limiting total carbohydrate intake, not sugar, to control blood glucose. Whether the carbohydrate is sugar or bread, it needs to be consumed in recommended amounts.

An individual's meal plan needs to be tailored to his or her type of diabetes, the treatment regime, and other health factors like obesity and blood lipids. Food preferences and lifestyle also need to be factored into the eating schedule.

Ten years ago sugar was restricted from the diabetic menu. Today, the glycemic index of foods has demonstrated how different foods affect blood glucose levels more than sugar. Carrots, corn flakes, and potatoes rank higher on the glycemic index, causing more elevated blood glucose levels than ice cream or a candy bar.

But sugar should not be added indiscriminately to the diet. Sweeteners should be used in small amounts and used in foods eaten as part of a meal. Sugary foods should not be eaten alone as a snack since this tends to raise blood glucose. When eaten as part of a balanced diet, sugar does not have the same blood glucose elevation effect as when it is eaten alone.

To eat the desserts featured in this cookbook, substitute a serving of your favorite recipe for another carbohydrate in your day's meal plan. Remember, the total amount of carbohydrates in the meal affects blood glucose management more than the source of the carbohydrate— simple sugar versus complex carbohydrates.*

---

*1994 Nutrition Recommendations for Diabetes, *Journal of the American Diabetes Association*, 94:507–11.

The American Diabetes Association dietary recommendations state that "scientific evidence has shown that the use of sucrose as part of the meal plan does not impair blood glucose control in individuals with Type I and Type II diabetes." But this does not mean you can eat desserts for breakfast, lunch, and dinner.

Calories and fat in the diet are important considerations when making food choices. Many desserts are loaded with fat which drives up the caloric content. These recipes are designed to provide good taste and enticing appearance while keeping sugar, calories, and fat to a reasonable level.

2

Cookies

Macadamia
White Chocolate Cookies

½ cup margarine or butter
¼ cup vegetable oil
2½ cups all-purpose flour
¾ cup brown sugar, packed firm
2 eggs
1 teaspoon vanilla extract
1 tablespoon baking powder
4 ounces white chocolate
    baking bar, chopped
1 3½ ounce jar macadamia nuts,
    chopped (¾ cup)

*P*reheat the oven to 375°F. Cream margarine or butter and oil together with an electric mixer. Add half of the flour and beat well. Mix in brown sugar, eggs, vanilla, and baking powder. Beat in remaining flour. Stir in white chocolate and nuts. Drop by rounded spoonfuls onto an ungreased baking sheet. Bake for 8 to 10 minutes, or until edges are lightly browned. Cool.

Makes 48 cookies
One serving of 1 cookie = 1 starch + 1 fat

Nutritive Values Per Serving

Calories	Carbohydrates	Protein	Fat	Sodium	Potassium	Cholesterol
90	12 g	1 g	6 g	28 mg	32 mg	8 mg

Chocolate Chip Cookies

¾ cup vegetable oil
¾ cup brown sugar, packed firm
1 egg
1⅔ cups all-purpose flour
2 teaspoons baking powder
½ cup semisweet chocolate chips
½ cup chopped walnuts

Preheat the oven to 375°F. Cream together oil, sugar, and egg. Add flour, baking powder, chips, and nuts. Mix well. Add 2 tablespoons water if batter does not stick together. Drop by spoonfuls onto a lightly oiled baking sheet. Bake for 10 to 15 minutes, or until golden brown.

Makes 36 cookies
One serving of 2 cookies = 1 starch + 2 fats

Nutritive Values Per Serving

Calories	Carbohydrates	Protein	Fat	Sodium	Potassium	Cholesterol
192	18 g	2 g	12 g	6 mg	70 mg	10 mg

Marsala Macaroons

4 egg whites
½ teaspoon cream of tartar
½ cup sugar
1 cup (almost 30) finely crushed
    vanilla wafers
¼ cup ground almonds
½ cup shredded coconut
1 tablespoon marsala or sweet sherry

*P*reheat the oven to 350°F. Beat egg whites with cream of tartar on high speed of an electric mixer until soft peaks form. Gradually add sugar and continue beating until stiff peaks form. Fold in vanilla wafer crumbs, almonds, coconut, and marsala. Spoon mixture onto a parchment-paper-lined baking pan leaving about one inch between cookies for spreading. Bake for 15 to 20 minutes, or until golden brown. Cool and store in an airtight container.

Makes 36 cookies
One serving of 2 cookies = 1 starch + 1 fat

Nutritive Values Per Serving

Calories	Carbohydrates	Protein	Fat	Sodium	Potassium	Cholesterol
82	11 g	2 g	4 g	62 mg	32 mg	0 mg

Gingersnaps

½ cup margarine or butter
¼ cup honey
⅓ cup molasses
1 egg
2 cups all-purpose flour
2 teaspoons ground ginger
1 teaspoon ground cinnamon
2 teaspoons baking powder
1 teaspoon baking soda

Cream together margarine or butter, honey, molasses, and egg. Mix together flour, ginger, cinnamon, baking powder, and baking soda. Add to creamed mixture. Beat well. Chill dough 1 hour. Preheat the oven to 350°F. Form dough into walnut-sized balls. Flatten slightly with the bottom of a small glass dipped in sugar and place on a lightly oiled baking sheet. Bake for 12 to 15 minutes, or until browned on edges.

Makes 36 cookies
One serving of 2 cookies = 1 starch + 1 fat

Nutritive Values Per Serving

Calories	Carbohydrates	Protein	Fat	Sodium	Potassium	Cholesterol
130	18 g	2 g	6 g	64 mg	110 mg	10 mg

Hazelnut Cookies

1 8-ounce package light cream cheese
3 tablespoons sugar
1 teaspoon vanilla extract
1 egg
1 cup all-purpose flour
1 teaspoon baking powder
¼ cup finely ground hazelnuts

Combine cream cheese, sugar, vanilla, and egg in mixing bowl. Beat until fluffy, at least 2 minutes. Add the rest of the ingredients. Mix well. Cover and refrigerate for at least 3 hours, or until thoroughly chilled. Preheat the oven to 325°F. Drop dough by teaspoonfuls onto an ungreased baking sheet. Bake for 15 to 20 minutes, or until browned. Cool.

Makes 36 cookies
One serving of 2 cookies = 1 starch + 2 fats

Nutritive Values Per Serving

Calories	Carbohydrates	Protein	Fat	Sodium	Potassium	Cholesterol
128	10 g	3 g	10 g	40 mg	54 mg	24 mg

Pumpkin Spice Cookies

¾ cup brown sugar, packed firm
½ cup vegetable oil
1 egg
8 ounces (1 cup) cooked or canned
    pumpkin
2 cups all-purpose flour
2 teaspoons baking powder
½ teaspoon baking soda
1 teaspoon ground cinnamon
¼ teaspoon ground nutmeg
½ teaspoon ground ginger
1 cup raisins

*P*reheat the oven to 375°F. Cream together sugar and oil. Add egg and pumpkin. Stir in flour, baking powder, baking soda, and spices. Add raisins and mix well. Drop by teaspoonfuls onto a lightly greased baking sheet. Bake for 15 to 20 minutes. Cool before storing in an air-tight container.

Makes 36 cookies
One serving of 1 cookie = 1 starch

Nutritive Values Per Serving

Calories	Carbohydrates	Protein	Fat	Sodium	Potassium	Cholesterol
80	12 g	1 g	3 g	4 mg	64 mg	5 mg

Chocolate Wafers

¼ cup margarine or butter
2 tablespoons sugar
1 egg
2 tablespoons cocoa
1 cup all-purpose flour
1 teaspoon baking powder
¼ teaspoon baking soda
2 tablespoons water
¼ cup finely chopped pecans

*B*eat together margarine or butter, sugar, egg, and cocoa. Add flour, baking powder, baking soda, and water. Mix well. Stir in pecans. Shape dough into a log 2 inches in diameter. Wrap in a cloth or plastic wrap. Refrigerate at least 2 hours or overnight.

Preheat the oven to 350°F. Slice dough into ½-inch-thick rounds and place on a lightly oiled baking sheet. Bake for 8 to 10 minutes. Cool thoroughly.

Makes 30 cookies
One serving of 2 cookies = ½ starch + 1 fat

Nutritive Values Per Serving

Calories	Carbohydrates	Protein	Fat	Sodium	Potassium	Cholesterol
82	9 g	1 g	5 g	40 mg	22 mg	12 mg

Biscotti Nut Cookies

1 cup hazelnuts
½ cup margarine or butter
¼ cup honey
2 eggs
1½ cups all-purpose flour
2 teaspoons baking powder

Preheat the oven to 350°F. Roast hazelnuts in oven just until browned. Cool enough to handle. Grind half of the nuts in a blender or nut chopper; leave remaining nuts whole. Beat margarine or butter, honey, and eggs together until light and fluffy. In a separate bowl, mix together flour, ground nuts, and baking powder. Gradually add flour mixture to creamed mixture. Beat on slow speed of an electric mixer until blended. Stir in whole nuts. Dough will be soft. Divide dough in half. Spoon onto a lightly oiled baking sheet, forming each half into a 12-inch-long strip, 2 to 2½ inches wide. Shape with a lightly floured spoon and your fingertips.

Bake for 15 minutes, or until golden brown. Remove from the oven and cut on a diagonal into ½-inch-thick slices. Turn each slice onto its side. Bake for 10 to 15 minutes longer, until toasted and golden. Cool completely on a wire rack.

Makes 48 cookies
One serving of 2 cookies = 1 starch + 1 fat

Nutritive Values Per Serving

Calories	Carbohydrates	Protein	Fat	Sodium	Potassium	Cholesterol
114	10 g	2 g	8 g	50 mg	42 mg	16 mg

Peanut Butter Cookies

¾ cup peanut butter
½ cup vegetable oil
½ cup brown sugar, packed firm
1 teaspoon vanilla extract
1 egg
1½ cups all-purpose flour
2 teaspoons baking powder
½ teaspoon baking soda

*P*reheat the oven to 350°F. Cream peanut butter, oil, sugar, vanilla, and egg together. Add remaining ingredients and beat well. Shape into 60 balls, 1 inch in diameter, and place on a lightly oiled baking sheet. Flatten with a fork or the bottom of a glass. Bake for 12 to 15 minutes, or until golden brown. Cool on rack.

Makes 60 small cookies
One serving of 2 cookies = 1 starch + 2 fats

Nutritive Values Per Serving

Calories	Carbohydrates	Protein	Fat	Sodium	Potassium	Cholesterol
174	4 g	4 g	2 g	54 mg	102 mg	10 mg

3

Bar Cookies

Strawberry Tea Bars

½ cup margarine or butter
¾ cup powdered sugar
1 egg
1 teaspoon almond extract
2 cups all-purpose flour
1 teaspoon baking powder
⅓ cup orange juice
½ cup all-fruit or low-sugar
    strawberry jam

*P*reheat the oven to 350°F. Beat margarine or butter, powdered sugar, egg, and almond extract together. Add flour, baking powder, and orange juice. Mix well. Spread dough in a lightly oiled 13″ × 9″ baking pan. Smooth jam over top of dough. Bake for 20 to 25 minutes, or until top is firm and edges are brown. Cool in the pan. Sprinkle with powdered sugar. Cut into 40 bars.

Makes 40 bars
One serving of 2 bars = 1 starch + 1 fat

Nutritive Values Per Serving

Calories	Carbohydrates	Protein	Fat	Sodium	Potassium	Cholesterol
120	18 g	2 g	4 g	62 mg	38 mg	10 mg

Apricot Oatmeal Squares

Apricot Filling
1½ cups dried apricot halves
½ cup water

Bottom Crust
⅓ cup margarine or butter
¼ cup brown sugar, packed firm
1 cup quick-cooking oatmeal
⅓ cup all-purpose flour
½ teaspoon ground cinnamon

Top Crust
1 egg
¼ cup brown sugar, packed firm
½ teaspoon baking powder
¼ cup diced roasted almonds
½ cup quick-cooking oatmeal
2 tablespoons all-purpose flour
¼ teaspoon ground nutmeg
½ cup water

*P*reheat the oven to 375°F. To make the filling, combine apricots and water in a small saucepan. Cook over medium heat in covered saucepan until apricots are tender. Puree in a blender or food processor.

Next, make the bottom crust by mixing margarine or butter, brown sugar, oatmeal, flour, and cinnamon together. Press into a 9″ × 13″ baking pan. Spread on apricot puree.

Combine the rest of the ingredients to make the top crust. Spoon over apricot filling. Bake for 30 to 35 minutes. Cool in the pan and slice into 30 squares.

Makes 30 bars
One serving of 1 bar = 1 starch

Nutritive Values Per Serving

Calories	Carbohydrates	Protein	Fat	Sodium	Potassium	Cholesterol
75	11 g	1.5 g	3 g	33 mg	171 mg	6 mg

Lemon Bars

Crust
⅓ cup margarine or butter
2 tablespoons powdered sugar
1 cup all-purpose flour

Topping
1½ teaspoons baking powder
¼ cup sugar
2 eggs
2 teaspoons grated lemon zest
1 tablespoon lemon juice
1 tablespoon all-purpose flour
Powdered sugar (garnish)

Preheat the oven to 350°F. Cream together margarine or butter and powdered sugar. Blend in flour and press into the bottom of a lightly oiled 8-inch square baking pan. Bake for 15 to 20 minutes, or until browned.

To make the topping, combine the rest of the ingredients, except powdered sugar, and pour evenly over baked crust. Bake 20 minutes longer. Cool in the pan. Cut into 16 squares. Sprinkle with powdered sugar.

Makes 16 bars
One serving of 1 bar = 1 starch + 1 fat

Nutritive Values Per Serving

Calories	Carbohydrates	Protein	Fat	Sodium	Potassium	Cholesterol
88	11 g	2 g	4 g	51 mg	18 mg	23 mg

Pineapple Cashew Brownies

2 cups all-purpose flour
⅔ cup cocoa
1 tablespoon baking powder
½ cup vegetable oil
⅓ cup honey
½ cup unsweetened applesauce
1 8-ounce can unsweetened
    crushed pineapple
½ cup chopped cashew pieces

*P*reheat the oven to 350°F. Combine flour, cocoa, and baking powder in a mixing bowl. Add the rest of the ingredients. Mix well. Pour batter into an oiled 9″ × 13″ baking pan. Bake for 25 to 30 minutes, or until brownies pull away from the sides of the pan. Cool in the pan and cut into 36 bars.

Makes 36 brownies
One serving of 1 brownie = 1 starch + 1 fat

Nutritive Values Per Serving

Calories	Carbohydrates	Protein	Fat	Sodium	Potassium	Cholesterol
82	11 g	1 g	4 g	3 mg	40 mg	1 mg

Fudge Brownies

¾ cup light brown sugar, packed firm
1 cup all-purpose flour
1 teaspoon baking soda
2 eggs
½ cup vegetable oil
¼ cup cocoa
¼ cup chopped pecans

Preheat the oven to 350°F. Combine all ingredients in a mixing bowl. Blend well. Spread into a well-oiled 9-inch square baking pan. Bake for 25 minutes, or until center is firm. Cool in the pan on a wire rack. Cut into 12 squares.

Makes 12 servings
One serving of 1 brownie = 1 starch + 2 fats

Nutritive Values Per Serving

Calories	Carbohydrates	Protein	Fat	Sodium	Potassium	Cholesterol
184	18 g	2 g	12 g	120 mg	71 mg	31 mg

Peppermint Brownies

1½ cups all-purpose flour
2 teaspoons baking powder
½ teaspoon baking soda
¾ cup sugar
½ cup vegetable oil
½ cup cocoa powder
2 eggs
¾ cup low-fat milk
1 teaspoon peppermint extract
1 cup chopped nuts
4 sugar-free round peppermint candies

*P*reheat the oven to 350°F. Combine all ingredients, except peppermint candies, in a mixing bowl. Mix until blended. Pour batter into a lightly oiled 9″ × 13″ baking pan. Bake for 20 to 30 minutes. While brownies are still hot, grind peppermint candies in a food processor or blender and sprinkle on top. Cool in the pan and cut into 30 bars.

Makes 30 brownies
One serving of 1 brownie = 1 starch + 1 fat

Nutritive Values Per Serving

Calories	Carbohydrates	Protein	Fat	Sodium	Potassium	Cholesterol
130	22 g	2 g	7 g	9 mg	49 mg	13 mg

4
Cakes

No-Bake Hazelnut Graham Cake

4 ounces semisweet chocolate, melted
¾ cup margarine or butter
½ cup powdered sugar
2 cups (about 16 squares) finely crushed
    graham crackers
⅔ cup coarsely chopped hazelnuts

Combine all ingredients. Mix well. Press into a lightly oiled springform pan. Chill at least 3 hours to set. Cut into 16 servings. Serve topped with fresh fruit and Raspberry Sauce (see Index).

Makes 16 servings
One serving of 1 piece = 1 starch + 3 fats

Nutritive Values Per Serving

Calories	Carbohydrates	Protein	Fat	Sodium	Potassium	Cholesterol
208	20 g	2 g	15 g	195 mg	110 mg	0 mg

Cookies and Cream Cheesecake

1 cup (almost 30) crushed
    vanilla wafers
2 tablespoons margarine or butter,
    melted
1 cup low-fat cottage cheese
1 cup low-fat sour cream
4 eggs, separated
1/3 cup sugar
1 cup low-fat cream cheese
1 teaspoon vanilla extract
1/2 cup (5 to 6 wafers) broken
    chocolate wafers
Chocolate curls
Fresh raspberries

*P*reheat the oven to 350°F. Combine vanilla wafer crumbs and margarine or butter in mixing bowl. Toss to blend well. Press into the bottom of a 10-inch springform pan. Mix together cottage cheese, sour cream, egg yolks, sugar, cream cheese, and vanilla in a food processor. Pour into a bowl. Beat egg whites on high speed of an electric mixer until stiff. Gently fold egg whites into cheese mixture. Pour batter into the springform pan. Drop chocolate wafer pieces into batter. Bake for 50 to 60 minutes, or until a knife inserted into the center comes out clean. *Do not overbake*. Cool in the pan. Chill at least 4 hours before serving. Garnish with chocolate curls and raspberries just before serving.

Makes 12 servings
One serving of 1 slice =
1 medium fat protein + 1 starch + 1 fruit + 2 fats

Nutritive Values Per Serving

Calories	Carbohydrates	Protein	Fat	Sodium	Potassium	Cholesterol
337	28 g	8 g	17 g	325 g	113 mg	115 mg

Applesauce Cake

2 apples, cored, peeled, and sliced
¼ cup apple juice or water
¼ cup sugar
½ teaspoon ground cinnamon
1 teaspoon grated lemon zest
¼ cup margarine or butter, softened
¼ cup brown sugar, packed firm
1 teaspoon vanilla extract
1 egg
2 cups all-purpose flour
1 tablespoon baking powder
1 teaspoon baking soda
¾ cup apple juice
½ cup chopped pecans
½ cup raisins
½ teaspoon ground nutmeg

*P*reheat the oven to 350°F. Put apples, apple juice, sugar, cinnamon, and lemon zest into a saucepan. Bring to boil, then reduce heat to simmer and cook until apples are tender, about 20 minutes. Mash to a smooth consistency. In a mixing bowl, cream together margarine or butter, brown sugar, vanilla, and egg. Add creamed mixture to apple mixture. Combine flour, baking powder, and baking soda in another bowl. Stir dry ingredients and ¾ cup apple juice into batter. Add pecans, raisins, and nutmeg. Beat well. Pour batter into a lightly oiled 13″ × 9″ baking pan. Bake for 40 to 50 minutes, or until a toothpick inserted into the center comes out clean. Cool in the pan and cut into 15 pieces.

Makes 15 servings
One serving of 1 piece = 1 starch + 1 fruit + 1 fat

Nutritive Values Per Serving

Calories	Carbohydrates	Protein	Fat	Sodium	Potassium	Cholesterol
175	28 g	3 g	6 g	127 mg	124 mg	17 mg

Orange Fig Cake

Cake
6 eggs, separated
½ cup sugar
1 cup all-purpose flour
1 teaspoon ground cinnamon
1 teaspoon baking powder
1 teaspoon grated orange zest
¼ cup orange juice
¼ teaspoon ground allspice
½ cup chopped almonds
10 dried figs, snipped into small pieces

Topping
2 tablespoons brown sugar
2 tablespoons orange juice
1 tablespoon margarine or butter
Orange slices

Preheat the oven to 350°F. Beat egg whites until stiff peaks form. In a separate mixing bowl, beat egg yolks with sugar until lemon colored. Add flour, cinnamon, baking powder, orange zest, orange juice, allspice, and almonds. Gently fold egg whites into cake mixture. Stir in figs. Pour into an ungreased 10-inch tube pan. Bake for 45 to 50 minutes. Cool for 5 minutes in the pan.

To make the topping, combine brown sugar, orange juice, and margarine or butter in saucepan. Cook on high heat for 2 to 3 minutes until margarine melts and mixture thickens. Pour evenly over cake. Cool thoroughly before cutting into 16 pieces and serving. Serve with orange slices as garnish on plate.

Makes 16 servings
One serving of 1 piece = 1 starch + 1 fat

Nutritive Values Per Serving

Calories	Carbohydrates	Protein	Fat	Sodium	Potassium	Cholesterol
139	22 g	4 g	5 g	31 mg	152 mg	69 mg

Poppy Seed Pound Cake

¾ cup margarine or butter
¾ cup sugar
3 eggs
1 teaspoon vanilla extract
¼ cup poppy seeds
1¼ cups all-purpose flour
2 teaspoons baking powder
1 teaspoon ground cinnamon

Preheat the oven to 350°F. Cream together margarine or butter and sugar. Add eggs, one at a time. Beat well. Add vanilla and poppy seeds. Combine flour, baking powder, and cinnamon in a separate mixing bowl. Stir to blend. Fold flour mixture into creamed mixture. Mix well. Spoon batter into a lightly oiled 9″ × 5″ loaf pan. Bake for 55 to 60 minutes, or until a toothpick inserted into the center comes out clean. Cool in the pan for 10 minutes before removing. Cool thoroughly and cut into 12 slices.

Makes 12 servings
One serving of 1 piece = 1 starch + 2 fats + 1 fruit

Nutritive Values Per Serving

Calories	Carbohydrates	Protein	Fat	Sodium	Potassium	Cholesterol
214	23 g	3 g	13 g	147 mg	33 mg	46 mg

Cappuccino Pudding Cake

1⅓ cups all-purpose flour
⅔ cup light brown sugar, packed firm
¼ cup cocoa
2 tablespoons instant coffee powder
2 teaspoons baking powder
½ teaspoon baking soda
1 egg
⅓ cup skim milk
2 tablespoons vegetable oil
¼ cup boiling water

Preheat the oven to 350°F. Combine flour, ⅓ cup of the brown sugar, 2 tablespoons of the cocoa, 1 tablespoon of the coffee powder, baking powder, and baking soda in a mixing bowl. Add egg, milk, and vegetable oil. Stir just until moistened. Pour batter into a lightly oiled 8-inch square baking pan. Combine remaining brown sugar, cocoa, and coffee powder. Sprinkle evenly over batter. Pour water evenly over batter. *Do not stir.* Bake for 25 to 30 minutes, or until a toothpick inserted in the center comes out clean. Cool in the pan and slice into 12 pieces.

Makes 12 servings
One serving of 1 piece = 1 starch + 1 fat

Nutritive Values Per Serving

Calories	Carbohydrates	Protein	Fat	Sodium	Potassium	Cholesterol
114	20 g	2 g	3 g	14 mg	69 mg	16 mg

Southern Pecan Oatmeal Cake

Cake

1½ cups boiling water
1 cup quick-cooking or regular oatmeal
½ cup margarine or butter, softened
½ cup brown sugar, packed firm
2 eggs
2 cups all-purpose flour
1 tablespoon baking powder
½ teaspoon baking soda
1 teaspoon ground cinnamon

Topping

2 tablespoons brown sugar
2 tablespoons margarine or butter,
    softened
2 tablespoons skim milk
¼ cup chopped pecans
¼ cup shredded coconut

*P*reheat the oven to 350°F. Pour boiling water over oatmeal. Add margarine or butter and let stand until melted. Stir in brown sugar, eggs, flour, baking powder, baking soda, and cinnamon. Pour batter into a lightly oiled 13" × 9" baking pan. Bake for 30 to 35 minutes, or until a toothpick inserted into the center comes out clean.

To make the topping, beat together brown sugar, margarine or butter, skim milk, pecans, and coconut. While cake is still warm, spread with topping mixture. Place cake with topping under the broiler until topping bubbles and toasts to a golden brown. Serve warm or cooled.

Makes 18 servings
One serving of 1 piece = 1 starch + 2 fats

Nutritive Values Per Serving

Calories	Carbohydrates	Protein	Fat	Sodium	Potassium	Cholesterol
169	20 g	3 g	9 g	122 mg	71 mg	20 mg

Carrot Cake

¼ cup chopped walnuts
¾ cup sugar
½ cup vegetable oil
2 eggs
1½ cups whole wheat flour
½ cup oatmeal
¼ cup wheat germ
1 tablespoon baking powder
1 teaspoon ground cinnamon
½ teaspoon ground nutmeg
1½ cups grated carrots
½ cup raisins
½ cup skim milk

Preheat the oven to 350°F. Oil and flour a 10-inch tube pan. Sprinkle in nuts. Combine sugar, oil, and eggs in a mixing bowl and beat well. Add the rest of the ingredients and mix until smooth. Pour batter into the pan. Bake for 50 to 60 minutes. Cool for 5 minutes in the pan before removing from the pan. Cool thoroughly before cutting into 15 slices.

Makes 15 servings
One serving of 1 piece = 1 starch + 1 fruit + 2 fats

Nutritive Values Per Serving

Calories	Carbohydrates	Protein	Fat	Sodium	Potassium	Cholesterol
218	29 g	5 g	10 g	17 mg	126 mg	25 mg

Chocolate Raisin Cake

½ cup cocoa
½ cup margarine or butter
¾ cup sugar
1 teaspoon grated orange zest
1 teaspoon vanilla extract
2 eggs
1½ cups all-purpose flour
2 teaspoons baking powder
½ teaspoon baking soda
¼ teaspoon salt
⅓ cup skim milk
½ cup chopped raisins or currants

Preheat the oven to 350°F. Combine cocoa, margarine or butter, sugar, orange zest, and vanilla in a saucepan. Heat over medium heat until margarine or butter is melted. Cool until lukewarm. Beat in the eggs, one at a time. Stir in flour, baking powder, baking soda, salt, and milk. Mix well. Stir in raisins and pour into a lightly oiled and floured 9″ × 5″ × 3″ loaf pan. Bake for 40 to 45 minutes. Cool for 5 minutes in the pan, then remove from the pan and cool on a wire rack. Cut into 12 slices.

Makes 12 servings
One serving of 1 piece = 1 starch + 1 fruit + 2 fats

Nutritive Values Per Serving

Calories	Carbohydrates	Protein	Fat	Sodium	Potassium	Cholesterol
214	31 g	3 g	9 g	156 mg	107 mg	32 mg

Caribbean Coconut Mousse Cake

Sponge Cake
6 eggs, separated
½ teaspoon cream of tartar
⅓ cup sugar
1 tablespoon lemon juice
½ cup water
1⅓ cups all-purpose flour
1 teaspoon baking powder
2 tablespoons toasted coconut

Mousse
15 ounces canned cream of coconut
1 package (0.3 ounces) sugar-free
    lemon gelatin
2 eggs
1 cup heavy whipping cream

Preheat the oven to 325°F. To make the cake, beat egg whites on high speed of an electric mixer until foamy. Add cream of tartar and continue beating until stiff but not dry. Beat egg yolks, sugar, and lemon juice together in a small bowl until light and fluffy, about 3 minutes at medium speed. Gradually add water, flour, and baking powder to egg yolk mixture. Continue beating for 2 minutes at medium speed. Fold egg whites into egg yolk batter gently but thoroughly. Pour batter into an ungreased 13" × 9" baking pan lined with waxed paper or parchment. Bake for 45 to 50 minutes, or until browned.

While the cake is baking, make the mousse. Combine cream of coconut, lemon gelatin, and eggs in a saucepan. Heat over medium heat, stirring constantly, until gelatin melts and small bubbles appear around the edges. Pour into a bowl and cool thoroughly (2 to 3 hours). Whip cream until soft peaks form. Fold cream into cooled cream of coconut mixture.

Cool cake thoroughly. Remove from pan and cut in half to form two layers. Spread half the mousse on the bottom layer. Place the top layer over the mousse. Cover top and sides with the rest of the mousse. Refrigerate at least 3 hours or overnight. Top with toasted coconut.

Makes 18 servings
One serving of 1 piece = 1 starch + 3 fats

Nutritive Values Per Serving

Calories	Carbohydrates	Protein	Fat	Sodium	Potassium	Cholesterol
207	14 g	5 g	16 g	33 mg	124 mg	99 mg

Peachy Upside-Down Cake

1 tablespoon margarine or butter
3 tablespoons brown sugar
4 ripe peaches, peeled and sliced
½ package (4 ounces) firm tofu,
    drained and cubed
1 cup apple juice
⅓ cup vegetable oil
⅓ cup sugar-free maple syrup
2 cups whole wheat flour
1 tablespoon baking powder
1½ teaspoons ground ginger
¼ teaspoon ground allspice
2 tablespoons grated orange zest

*P*reheat the oven to 350°F. Melt margarine or butter in the bottom of an 8-inch square pan and rub onto sides. Sprinkle brown sugar into the bottom of the pan. Arrange peach slices over brown sugar. Combine tofu, juice, oil, and syrup in a food processor or blender. Process just until smooth. Pour into a mixing bowl. Add flour, baking powder, ginger, allspice, and orange zest. Beat with a wooden spoon until batter is smooth. Pour batter over peach slices. Bake for 30 to 40 minutes, or until a toothpick inserted into the center comes out clean. Cool for 5 minutes, then invert onto a serving plate to cool thoroughly. Slice into 8 pieces.

Makes 8 servings
One serving of 1 piece = 1 starch + 2 fruits

Nutritive Values Per Serving

Calories	Carbohydrates	Protein	Fat	Sodium	Potassium	Cholesterol
273	36 g	7 g	12 g	22 mg	183 mg	0 mg

Pineapple Upside-Down Cake

8 canned pineapple rings *or*
    ½ cup (4 ounces) canned
    pineapple chunks (packed in juice)
2 tablespoons molasses
⅓ cup margarine or butter
½ cup honey
2 eggs
1½ cups all-purpose flour
½ teaspoon baking soda
¾ cup pineapple juice (reserved from
    pineapple—add water if not enough juice)

*P*reheat the oven to 350°F. Liberally oil a 9-inch square baking pan. Arrange pineapple rings or chunks in the bottom of the pan. Drizzle on molasses. Beat together margarine or butter, honey, and eggs. Add the rest of the ingredients and stir until smooth. Pour batter over the pineapple. Bake for 30 to 35 minutes. Cool at least 30 minutes before serving. May be served hot or cold. Cut into 12 squares.

Makes 12 servings

One serving of 1 square = 1 starch + 1 fruit + 1 fat

Nutritive Values Per Serving

Calories	Carbohydrates	Protein	Fat	Sodium	Potassium	Cholesterol
180	30 g	3 g	6 g	71 mg	118 mg	30 mg

Deviled Angel Food Cake

12 egg whites
1½ teaspoons cream of tartar
¾ cup sugar
½ cup cocoa
1 cup all-purpose flour

Preheat the oven to 350°F. Egg whites need to be at room temperature for best results. Sprinkle cream of tartar over egg whites and beat at high speed of an electric mixer until soft peaks form. Slowly add sugar and continue beating until stiff peaks form. Sift together cocoa and flour and sprinkle over egg white mixture. Fold in with a wire whip until all flour is incorporated. *Do not overbeat.* Pour batter into a 10-inch angel food pan. Bake for 30 to 35 minutes, or until top is dry and bounces back when touched. Allow cake to cool in the pan, inverted on a wire rack. Use a knife or metal spatula to loosen cake from the sides of the pan before removing pan. Cool. Cut into 12 pieces and serve with Fruit Sauce (see Index).

Makes 12 servings
One serving of 1 piece with sauce = 1 starch + 1 fruit

Nutritive Values Per Serving

Calories	Carbohydrates	Protein	Fat	Sodium	Potassium	Cholesterol
139	26 g	6 g	2 g	81 mg	121 mg	1 mg

Fruit Sauce

2 tablespoons margarine or butter
¼ cup sugar
1 cup evaporated skim milk
1 tablespoon cornstarch
½ teaspoon vanilla extract
1 cup fresh raspberries or strawberries

Combine all ingredients, except vanilla extract and fruit, in a saucepan. Cook over medium heat until mixture bubbles around the edges. Remove from heat. Add vanilla. Pour into a bowl and let stand until cool. Add fruit and stir to blend.

Makes about 1½ cups sauce
One serving of 2 tablespoons = ½ fruit

Nutritive Values Per Serving

Calories	Carbohydrates	Protein	Fat	Sodium	Potassium	Cholesterol
28	4 g	1 g	1 g	23 mg	44 mg	0 mg

Fresh Orange Torte

2 cups all-purpose flour
1 tablespoon baking powder
¾ cup sugar
¾ cup margarine or butter
Grated zest of 1 orange
3 eggs
¾ cup orange juice

Preheat the oven to 350°F. Stir together flour and baking powder. In another bowl, cream together sugar, margarine or butter, and orange zest. Add one egg at a time and beat well. Add flour mixture and orange juice to creamed mixture. Stir until batter is smooth. Pour batter into two oiled and floured 8-inch round cake pans. Bake for 25 to 30 minutes or until a toothpick inserted into the center comes out clean. Cool for 5 minutes on a wire rack before removing from the pan. When thoroughly cool, spread one layer with Creamy Orange Icing (see Index). Top with second layer and frost top and sides. Cut into 16 slices.

Makes 16 servings
One serving of 1 piece with icing = 2 starches + 2 fats

Nutritive Values Per Serving

Calories	Carbohydrates	Protein	Fat	Sodium	Potassium	Cholesterol
295	39 g	11 g	11 g	231 mg	399 mg	45 mg

Creamy Orange Icing

1 cup instant nonfat dry milk
3 egg whites
½ teaspoon cream of tartar
¼ cup powdered sugar
1 teaspoon pure orange extract

*P*lace dry milk in a blender and puree until granules are fine. Beat egg whites with cream of tartar on high speed of an electric mixer until frothy. Gradually add sugar and dry milk. Continue beating while adding orange extract. Mix until thick. Spread on cooled Fresh Orange Torte (see Index).

Makes 2 cups

Killer Chocolate Cake

1½ cups all-purpose flour
¾ cup sugar
1 teaspoon baking soda
2 teaspoons baking powder
½ cup cocoa
½ cup vegetable oil
2 ounces sweet baking chocolate, melted
1 cup milk
2 eggs
1 ounce finely chopped semisweet baking
    chocolate *or* ¼ cup mini chocolate chips

Preheat the oven to 350°F. Stir together flour, sugar, baking soda, baking powder, and cocoa. Add oil, sweet chocolate, and milk. Beat 2 minutes at medium speed with an electric mixer or 300 strokes by hand. Add eggs. Beat 2 more minutes or 300 strokes. Sprinkle semisweet chocolate over batter. Stir to blend. Pour batter into two oiled and floured 8-inch round cake pans. Bake for 25 to 30 minutes or until a toothpick inserted into the center comes out clean. Cool for 5 minutes on a wire rack before removing from the pan. When completely cool, spread one layer with White Chocolate Icing (see Index). Top with second layer and frost top and sides. Cut into 16 pieces.

Makes 16 servings
One serving of 1 piece with icing =
1 starch + 2 fruits + 2 fats

Nutritive Values Per Serving

Calories	Carbohydrates	Protein	Fat	Sodium	Potassium	Cholesterol
265	34 g	8 g	11 g	326 mg	280 mg	28 mg

White Chocolate Icing

1 cup instant nonfat dry milk
3 egg whites
½ teaspoon cream of tartar
¼ cup powdered sugar
2 ounces white chocolate, grated

Place dry milk crystals in a blender (do not add water). Blend to make fine-textured crystals. Set aside for later use. Beat egg whites and cream of tartar on high speed of an electric mixer until frothy. Gradually beat in sugar. Add dry milk gradually and beat until creamy. Spread onto cooled cake. Sprinkle white chocolate on top of icing.

Makes enough icing for an 8-inch two-layer cake

Banana Dream Cake

½ cup margarine or butter
¾ cup sugar
2 eggs
2 bananas
2½ cups all-purpose flour
1 tablespoon baking powder
1 teaspoon ground cinnamon
½ teaspoon ground nutmeg
¾ cup milk chocolate chips
1 cup apple juice

Preheat the oven to 350°F. Combine margarine or butter, sugar, eggs, and bananas in a food processor or blender. Blend well and pour into a mixing bowl. Add the rest of the ingredients, except ¼ cup milk chocolate chips. Stir to mix well. Pour into a well-oiled 10-inch tube pan. Bake for 40 to 50 minutes. Cool for 5 minutes in the pan. Invert on a serving plate and remove the pan. Top with remaining chocolate chips. Cool thoroughly before cutting into 16 slices and serving.

Makes 16 servings
One serving of 1 piece = 1 starch + 1 fruit + 2 fats

Nutritive Values Per Serving

Calories	Carbohydrates	Protein	Fat	Sodium	Potassium	Cholesterol
232	35 g	4 g	9 g	83 mg	141 mg	34 mg

5

Pies and Pastries

Apple and Cheese Pie

3 large tart apples, peeled and sliced
1 tablespoon sugar
1 tablespoon all-purpose flour
½ teaspoon ground nutmeg
1 cup shredded cheddar cheese
½ cup all-purpose flour
1 tablespoon brown sugar
2 tablespoons margarine or butter
1 unbaked 9-inch pie shell

*P*reheat the oven to 400°F. Put apples into a bowl. Sprinkle on sugar, 1 tablespoon flour, and nutmeg. Spread apple mixture into the pie shell and cover with cheese. Mix ½ cup flour, brown sugar, and margarine or butter with a fork to a crumbly consistency. Sprinkle mixture over cheese and bake for 30 to 40 minutes, or until apples are tender. Cool slightly and cut into 8 slices. Serve warm or cold.

Makes 8 servings
One serving of 1 slice = 1 starch + 1 fruit + 3 fats

Nutritive Values Per Serving

Calories	Carbohydrates	Protein	Fat	Sodium	Potassium	Cholesterol
276	30 g	6 g	15 g	246 mg	119 mg	15 mg

Key Lime Pie

1½ cups (about 24 squares)
    graham cracker crumbs
4 tablespoons margarine or butter,
    melted
3 eggs, separated
12-ounce-can evaporated skim milk
1 tablespoon cornstarch
⅓ cup sugar
⅓ cup fresh lime juice
2–3 drops green food color (optional)
¼ cup sugar
Lime slices

*P*reheat the oven to 350°F. Combine graham cracker crumbs and margarine or butter in a bowl. Toss to blend. Press into the bottom and sides of a 9-inch pie pan. Bake for 7 to 10 minutes, or until browned. Combine egg yolks, milk, cornstarch, and ⅓ cup sugar in a saucepan. Cook over medium heat, stirring constantly, until mixture comes to a full rolling boil. Remove from heat. Stir in lime juice and, if a green-tinted filling is desired, food color. Pour mixture into graham cracker crust. Let cool. Meanwhile, beat egg whites with an electric mixer until frothy. Gradually add ¼ cup sugar and beat until stiff peaks form. Spoon meringue over filling. Bake for 3 minutes, or until edges are browned. Cool thoroughly before cutting into 9 slices and serving. Garnish with lime slices.

Makes 9 servings
One serving of 1 slice = 2 starches + 1 fat

Nutritive Values Per Serving

Calories	Carbohydrates	Protein	Fat	Sodium	Potassium	Cholesterol
232	34 g	6 g	8 g	249 mg	182 mg	62 mg

Poppy Seed Crumble

Bottom Crust
¾ cup all-purpose flour
2 tablespoons baking powder
¼ cup powdered sugar
1 egg
1 teaspoon vanilla extract
2 tablespoons margarine or butter, softened
¼ cup no-sugar-added strawberry jam

Filling
¼ cup poppy seeds
½ cup skim milk
1 tablespoon margarine or butter
¼ cup all-purpose flour
1 tablespoon sugar
1 egg
½ teaspoon grated lemon zest

Topping
½ cup all-purpose flour
2 tablespoons powdered sugar
2 tablespoons margarine or butter
½ teaspoon ground cinnamon

*P*reheat the oven to 375°F. To make the bottom crust, combine flour, baking powder, powdered sugar, egg, vanilla, and margarine or butter. Beat well. With lightly floured hands, press dough evenly into an oiled 8-inch square pan. Bake for 8 to 10 minutes. Heat strawberry jam to melt. Spread over crust.

Make the poppy seed filling by combining poppy seeds, milk, margarine or butter, flour, sugar, egg, and lemon zest in a bowl. Pour over crust.

To make the topping, combine flour, powdered sugar, margarine or butter, and cinnamon. Stir with fork until texture is crumbly. Sprinkle topping over poppy seed filling. Bake for 20 to 30 minutes, or until a toothpick inserted into the center comes out clean. Cool thoroughly and cut into 9 servings.

Makes 9 servings
One serving of 1 square = 1 starch + 1 fruit + 1 fat

Nutritive Values Per Serving

Calories	Carbohydrates	Protein	Fat	Sodium	Potassium	Cholesterol
197	28 g	4 g	8 g	103 mg	76 mg	49 mg

Chocolate Apple Delight

Pastry
1 cup all-purpose flour
2 tablespoons cocoa
1 teaspoon baking powder
½ teaspoon baking soda
½ cup unsweetened applesauce
¼ cup honey
1 egg
3 tablespoons vegetable oil
½ cup skim milk

Topping
2 cups peeled, sliced apples
  (2 medium apples)
½ cup apple juice
1 tablespoon cornstarch
3 tablespoons water
½ teaspoon ground cinnamon
2 teaspoons sugar

Preheat the oven to 350°F. Combine flour, cocoa, baking powder, and baking soda in a mixing bowl. Stir to blend. Add applesauce, honey, egg, oil, and milk. Mix well. Pour batter into an oiled 8-inch square baking pan. Bake for 20 to 30 minutes, or until a toothpick inserted into the center comes out clean.

Let pastry cool while making apple topping. Combine apples and apple juice in a saucepan. Cover and cook over medium heat for 3 to 4 minutes, or until apples are tender. Mix cornstarch and water together. Pour into pan with apples and cook 1 minute, or until thickened. Cool 10 to 15 minutes. Spread topping over pastry. Mix cinnamon and sugar together. Sprinkle over top of apples. Cool before cutting into 9 squares and serving.

Makes 9 servings
One serving of 1 square = 1 starch + 1 fruit + 1 fat

Nutritive Values Per Serving

Calories	Carbohydrates	Protein	Fat	Sodium	Potassium	Cholesterol
175	29 g	3 g	6 g	89 mg	119 mg	29 mg

Mud Pie

Crust
1½ cups (50 wafers) crushed vanilla wafers
3 tablespoons margarine or butter, melted

Filling
1 pint low-fat chocolate ice cream
1 quart low-fat coffee ice cream

Caramel Sauce
¼ cup butterscotch chips
1 tablespoon low-fat milk

Mix vanilla wafers with margarine or butter. Press into the bottom of a 9-inch pie plate. Spread chocolate ice cream on crust. Scoop coffee ice cream over chocolate layer. Place in freezer.

Make caramel sauce by melting butterscotch chips and milk. Stir to mix. Cool to refrigerator temperature. Spoon over coffee ice cream mounds. Return to freezer and freeze at least 3 hours before serving. Cut into 10 slices.

Makes 10 servings
One serving of 1 slice = 2 starches + 4 fats

Nutritive Values Per Serving

Calories	Carbohydrates	Protein	Fat	Sodium	Potassium	Cholesterol
327	38 g	6 g	19 g	248 mg	204 mg	120 mg

Rhubarb Crumble

3 cups chopped fresh or frozen rhubarb
½ cup orange juice
3 tablespoons all-purpose flour
1 egg
⅓ cup brown sugar, packed firm
½ teaspoon ground cinnamon
2 tablespoons margarine or butter
¼ cup oatmeal

Preheat the oven to 350°F. Put rhubarb in a 1½-quart casserole dish. Combine orange juice, flour, and egg in a bowl. Beat well. Pour over rhubarb. In a separate bowl, mix together brown sugar, cinnamon, margarine or butter, and oatmeal using a fork. Sprinkle topping over rhubarb mixture. Bake for 25 to 30 minutes or until fruit is tender. Divide into 4 portions and serve hot or cold.

Makes 4 servings
One serving = 1 starch + 1 fruit + 1 fat

Nutritive Values Per Serving

Calories	Carbohydrates	Protein	Fat	Sodium	Potassium	Cholesterol
193	27 g	4 g	8 g	95 mg	410 mg	65 mg

Cream Puffs

Pastry Puffs
½ cup water
¼ cup margarine or butter
½ cup all-purpose flour
Pinch of salt
2 eggs

Custard Filling
2 cups skim milk
2 tablespoons cornstarch
2 eggs
Pinch of salt
⅓ cup sugar
1 teaspoon vanilla extract

Chocolate Topping
¼ cup semisweet chocolate chips
1 teaspoon margarine or butter
1 teaspoon water

*P*reheat the oven to 425°F. To make the pastry puffs, heat the water and margarine or butter in a saucepan until water boils and margarine is melted. Add flour and salt. Heat thoroughly. Stir while cooking over a low flame until mixture forms a stiff ball. Remove mixture from heat and add eggs, one at a time. Beat well. Drop by teaspoonfuls onto an ungreased baking sheet. Bake for 15 minutes. Then reduce heat to 325 degrees and bake for 20 minutes. Let cool on a wire rack.

Next, make the custard filling. Pour milk into a saucepan. Sprinkle cornstarch on top. Add the rest of the ingredients, except the vanilla extract, and stir to dissolve the cornstarch. Heat mixture over medium heat, stirring constantly, until mixture thickens. Bring to a boil for 1 minute. Remove from heat and stir in the vanilla. Cool in the refrigerator, at least 30 minutes.

While custard cools, make the chocolate topping. Combine chocolate chips, margarine or butter, and water in a saucepan. Melt chocolate over low heat until smooth.

Cut a hole in the top of each cream puff. Spoon cooled custard into each cream puff and return the top to each puff. Drizzle warm chocolate topping over each. Refrigerate cream puffs until ready to serve.

Makes 4 servings
One serving of 1 cream puff = 1 starch +
½ low-fat milk + 1 fat

Nutritive Values Per Serving

Calories	Carbohydrates	Protein	Fat	Sodium	Potassium	Cholesterol
226	24 g	6 g	12 g	140 mg	180 mg	98 mg

Fruit Tart

1 cup flour
¼ teaspoon salt
¼ cup margarine or butter
2 tablespoons water
Custard filling (see Index)
1½ cups sliced fruit—kiwi, strawberries,
    peaches, or nectarines

Preheat oven to 400°F. Combine flour, salt, and margarine or butter in a mixing bowl. Mix with a fork or pastry blender until crumbly. Add water. Stir until mixture forms a ball. Place on a lightly floured pastry cloth and roll out large enough to fill an 8-inch pie pan or divide dough into 8 portions for individual tarts. Roll each portion on a lightly floured surface and fit into muffin cups or a tart pan. Flute edges. Bake 8 to 10 minutes, or until browned. Prick with a fork if crust bubbles up during baking. Cool.

Fill with custard filling. Top with fresh fruit slices. Chill until ready to serve.

Makes 8 servings
One serving = 1 starch + 1 fruit + 2 fats

Nutritive Values Per Serving

Calories	Carbohydrates	Protein	Fat	Sodium	Potassium	Cholesterol
249	28 g	5 g	12 g	384 mg	711 mg	79 mg

Apple Cobbler

4 apples, peeled and sliced
3 tablespoons sugar
1 tablespoon tapioca or flour
½ teaspoon ground cinnamon
¼ teaspoon ground nutmeg
1 cup flour
1½ teaspoons baking powder
4 tablespoons margarine or butter
¼ cup skim milk

Preheat the oven to 375°F. Put apples into a 1½-quart baking dish. Blend together sugar, tapioca or flour, cinnamon, and nutmeg. Sprinkle over the apple slices. Combine 1 cup flour and baking powder in a mixing bowl. Stir to blend. Cut in margarine or butter. Stir in milk and beat until mixture forms a ball. Press dough out onto a floured surface and into the shape of the baking dish. Place dough on top of apple slices. Bake for 30 minutes, or until pastry is browned. Cool and divide into 6 servings. Serve warm or cold.

Makes 6 servings
One serving = 2 fruits + 1 starch

Nutritive Values Per Serving

Calories	Carbohydrates	Protein	Fat	Sodium	Potassium	Cholesterol
225	36 g	3 g	8 g	95 mg	141 mg	0 mg

6

Muffins and Quick Breads

Gingerbread Muffins

1 cup all-purpose flour
¼ cup molasses
⅓ cup buttermilk
2 tablespoons vegetable oil
2 tablespoons sugar
1 egg
½ teaspoon ground cinnamon
½ teaspoon ground ginger
¼ teaspoon ground cloves
1 teaspoon baking powder
½ teaspoon baking soda
¼ cup dried figs, snipped into
    small pieces
Powdered sugar (optional)

*P*reheat the oven to 400°F. Combine all ingredients except powdered sugar in a mixing bowl. Stir to blend. Spoon into prepared muffin cups or an oiled muffin tin. Bake for 15 to 20 minutes, or until a toothpick inserted in the center comes out clean. Cool. Dust with powdered sugar, if desired.

Makes 8 muffins
One serving of 1 muffin = 1 starch + 1 fruit + 1 fat

Nutritive Values Per Serving

Calories	Carbohydrates	Protein	Fat	Sodium	Potassium	Cholesterol
162	28 g	3 g	4 g	23 mg	252 mg	23 mg

Rhubarb Walnut Muffins

½ cup whole wheat flour
¼ cup sugar
1 tablespoon baking powder
½ teaspoon ground cinnamon
1 cup finely chopped fresh or frozen rhubarb
¼ cup chopped walnuts
½ cup skim milk
1 egg
2 tablespoons vegetable oil

*P*reheat the oven to 350°F. Stir together flour, sugar, baking powder, and cinnamon. Add rhubarb and nuts. In another bowl, combine milk, egg, and oil. Pour milk mixture into other ingredients. Mix just until dry ingredients are moistened. Spoon batter into prepared muffin cups or an oiled muffin tin. Bake for 20 to 25 minutes.

Makes 8 muffins
One serving of 1 muffin = 1 starch + 1 fruit + 1 fat

Nutritive Values Per Serving

Calories	Carbohydrates	Protein	Fat	Sodium	Potassium	Cholesterol
181	27 g	4 g	7 g	16 mg	120 mg	23 mg

Pumpkin Date Muffins

1 cup all-purpose flour
2 tablespoons sugar
2 teaspoons baking powder
½ teaspoon baking soda
½ teaspoon ground cinnamon
¼ teaspoon ground nutmeg
½ cup orange juice
2 tablespoons vegetable oil
1 egg
4 ounces (½ cup) cooked or canned pumpkin
½ cup chopped dates

*P*reheat the oven to 400°F. Combine the flour, sugar, baking powder, baking soda, cinnamon, and nutmeg in a bowl. Blend thoroughly. Add the orange juice, oil, egg, pumpkin, and dates. Stir just until the dry ingredients are mixed. Pour into prepared muffin cups or a lightly oiled muffin tin. Bake for about 15 minutes.

Makes 8 servings
One serving of 1 muffin = 1 starch + 1 fruit + 1 fat

Nutritive Values Per Serving

Calories	Carbohydrates	Protein	Fat	Sodium	Potassium	Cholesterol
151	27 g	3 g	4 g	9 mg	157 mg	23 mg

Sour Cream Coffee Cake

½ cup margarine or butter
¾ cup sugar
1 egg
1½ cups all-purpose flour
2 teaspoons baking powder
1 teaspoon baking soda
½ teaspoon salt
1 cup low-fat sour cream
1 teaspoon vanilla extract
2 tablespoons sugar
1 teaspoon ground cinnamon
¼ cup finely chopped walnuts

Preheat the oven to 350°F. Cream together margarine or butter and ¾ cup sugar. Add egg and beat well. Combine flour, baking powder, baking soda, and salt in another bowl. Stir to mix. Add flour mixture to creamed mixture, alternating with sour cream and vanilla. Pour batter into a well-oiled 13″ × 9″ baking pan. Combine 2 tablespoons sugar, cinnamon, and walnuts. Sprinkle evenly over top of batter. Bake for 30 to 45 minutes, or until a toothpick inserted into the center comes out clean. Cool. Cut into 18 squares and serve warm or cold.

Makes 18 servings
One serving of 1 square = 1 starch + 2 fats

Nutritive Values Per Serving

Calories	Carbohydrates	Protein	Fat	Sodium	Potassium	Cholesterol
162	19 g	2 g	9 g	136 mg	46 mg	10 mg

Pumpkin Raisin Bread

½ cup vegetable oil
¼ cup sugar
2 eggs
6 ounces (¾ cup) cooked or canned pumpkin
2 cups all-purpose flour
1 tablespoon baking powder
½ teaspoon baking soda
1 teaspoon ground cinnamon
½ cup dark or golden raisins
¼ cup orange juice

Preheat the oven to 350°F. Beat together oil, sugar, eggs, and pumpkin until light and fluffy. Combine flour, baking powder, baking soda, cinnamon, and raisins in a bowl. Add creamed mixture and orange juice. Pour into an oiled 9" × 5" loaf pan. Bake for 40 to 45 minutes. Cool at least 30 minutes before slicing.

Makes 15 servings
One serving of 1 slice = 1 starch + 2 fats

Nutritive Values Per Serving

Calories	Carbohydrates	Protein	Fat	Sodium	Potassium	Cholesterol
167	22 g	3 g	8 g	9 mg	94 mg	24 mg

Banana Bread

2 cups whole wheat flour
1 tablespoon baking powder
1 teaspoon ground cinnamon
½ teaspoon ground nutmeg
2 eggs
½ cup vegetable oil
3 tablespoons sugar
2 large ripe bananas
3 tablespoons frozen orange juice
    concentrate, thawed
1 tablespoon grated orange zest

Preheat the oven to 350°F. Combine flour, baking powder, cinnamon, and nutmeg in a mixing bowl. Puree eggs, oil, sugar, bananas, orange juice concentrate, and orange zest in a food processor or blender until smooth. Pour into flour mixture. Mix well. Pour batter into an oiled 9" × 5" loaf pan. Bake for 45 to 55 minutes. Cool on a wire rack for 10 minutes before removing from the pan. Cut into 15 slices.

Makes 15 servings
One serving of 1 slice = 1 starch + 1 fat

Nutritive Values Per Serving

Calories	Carbohydrates	Protein	Fat	Sodium	Potassium	Cholesterol
157	18 g	3 g	8 g	9 mg	95 mg	29 mg

7

Holiday Favorites

Pumpkin Cheesecake

2 tablespoons margarine or butter
¼ cup graham cracker crumbs
16 ounces (2 cups) dry cottage cheese,
    pureed in blender
½ cup brown sugar, packed firm
3 eggs
1 teaspoon ground cinnamon
½ teaspoon ground nutmeg
16 ounces (2 cups) canned or cooked pumpkin
Fresh orange sections
Chopped pecans

Preheat the oven to 350°F. Spread margarine or butter over bottom and sides of a springform pan or an 8-inch square baking pan. Sprinkle on graham cracker crumbs. Combine other ingredients, except orange sections and pecans, in a bowl and beat until smooth and fluffy. Pour mixture into the prepared pan and bake for 45 minutes. Cool on a wire rack and top with orange sections and chopped pecans before cutting into 12 slices and serving.

Makes 12 servings
One serving of 1 slice = 1 starch + ½ fat

Nutritive Values Per Serving

Calories	Carbohydrates	Protein	Fat	Sodium	Potassium	Cholesterol
97	11 g	6 g	3 g	55 mg	134 mg	47 mg

Pecan Tea Crescent

1 package (1 tablespoon) active dry yeast
¼ cup warm water (110° to 115°F)
2 cups all-purpose flour
3 tablespoons sugar
¼ teaspoon salt
¾ cup margarine or butter
¼ cup evaporated low-fat milk
1 egg
½ cup golden raisins
⅓ cup finely chopped pecans
1 tablespoon brown sugar
¼ cup all-fruit apricot jam

Dissolve yeast in water. Combine flour, sugar, and salt in a mixing bowl. Cut in ½ cup margarine or butter with a pastry blender until mixture resembles pie crust. Add milk, egg, raisins, and yeast mixture. Mix well. Cover and chill at least 4 hours, or overnight. Roll dough out onto a floured surface and into a 12″ × 18″ rectangle. Spread with ¼ cup margarine, pecans, and brown sugar. Roll up into a log. Place on a lightly oiled baking sheet in the shape of a crescent. Make cuts along outside edge about one inch apart. Give each section a half turn so that a cut edge rests on the baking sheet.

Cover crescent and let rise in a warm place (about 100°F) for 30 minutes.

Preheat the oven to 350°F. Bake for 30 to 35 minutes, or until golden brown. Glaze with apricot jam and slice into 24 pieces.

Makes 24 servings
One serving of 1 piece = 1 bread + 1 fat

Nutritive Values Per Serving

Calories	Carbohydrates	Protein	Fat	Sodium	Potassium	Cholesterol
124	16 g	2 g	7 g	98 mg	64 mg	8 mg

Chocolate Swirl Brioche

1 package (1 tablespoon active) dry yeast
¼ cup warm milk (80° to 85°F)
1 tablespoon sugar
2 eggs
¼ cup margarine or butter, softened
About 2 cups all-purpose flour
½ cup milk chocolate chips, melted
Powdered sugar

Dissolve yeast in milk. Beat sugar, eggs, margarine or butter, and 1 cup flour together. Add yeast mixture. Beat well for 3 minutes on medium speed of an electric mixer. Beat in another ½ cup flour. Turn out onto a surface floured with remaining ½ cup flour and knead to form a smooth pliable dough, about 10 minutes by hand. Dough will be sticky at first but will change while kneading. Shape dough into a ball. Place in a plastic bag, seal bag, and allow to rest in a warm place for 20 minutes.

Turn dough onto a lightly floured surface. Punch down by kneading briefly. Roll out dough into a 12″ × 6″ rectangle. Spread melted chocolate onto dough. Roll up jelly-roll fashion. Place on a lightly oiled baking sheet in a ring. With a sharp knife, cut 1-inch-deep slashes into the top of the ring, about 2 inches apart. Cover and set in a warm place to rise for about 40 minutes, or until doubled in size.

Preheat the oven to 350°F. Bake for 20 to 25 minutes. Cool on a wire rack and dust lightly with powdered sugar. Cut into 12 pieces.

Makes 12 servings
One serving of 1 piece = 1 starch + 1 fat

Nutritive Values Per Serving

Calories	Carbohydrates	Protein	Fat	Sodium	Potassium	Cholesterol
167	22 g	4 g	7 g	61 mg	108 mg	32 mg

Chocolate Cinnamon Crescent

1 package (1 tablespoon) active dry yeast
¼ cup warm water (110° to 115°F)
1⅔ cups whole wheat flour
⅓ cup cocoa
½ cup sugar
¼ teaspoon salt
½ cup margarine or butter
¼ cup skim milk
1 egg
½ cup chopped walnuts
1 teaspoon ground cinnamon
Powdered sugar

Dissolve yeast in water. Combine flour, cocoa, ¼ cup sugar, and salt in a mixing bowl. Cut in margarine or butter until mixture is crumbly. Add yeast, milk, egg, and nuts. Mix well. Cover and refrigerate at least 3 hours or overnight.

Roll dough out onto a surface coated with cocoa and form into a 12″ × 6″ rectangle. Combine remaining ¼ cup sugar and cinnamon in a bowl. Sprinkle over dough. Roll up and shape into a crescent on a lightly greased baking sheet. Make cuts along the edges about 1 inch apart and to within ½ inch of center. Give each section a half turn so that a cut edge rests on the baking sheet. Let rise in a warm place about 30 minutes.

Preheat the oven to 350°F. Bake for 20 to 25 minutes, or until browned on edges. Dust with powdered sugar and cut into 16 pieces.

Makes 16 servings
One serving of 1 piece = 1 starch + 2 fats

Nutritive Values Per Serving

Calories	Carbohydrates	Protein	Fat	Sodium	Potassium	Cholesterol
117	9 g	2 g	8 g	111 mg	52 mg	12 mg

Pumpkin Pie

16 ounces (2 cups) canned or cooked pumpkin
2 eggs
¼ cup honey
1 cup evaporated skim milk
1½ teaspoons ground cinnamon
½ teaspoon ground nutmeg
¼ teaspoon ground cloves
1 unbaked 9-inch pie shell

*P*reheat the oven to 375°F. Beat pumpkin, eggs, honey, milk, cinnamon, nutmeg, and cloves together. Pour into pie shell. Bake for 50 to 60 minutes, or until a knife inserted into the center comes out clean. Cool thoroughly and cut into 12 slices.

Makes 12 servings
One serving of 1 slice = 1 starch + 1 fat

Nutritive Values Per Serving

Calories	Carbohydrates	Protein	Fat	Sodium	Potassium	Cholesterol
134	18 g	4 g	6 g	122 mg	174 mg	31 mg

Mincemeat Pie

5 cups finely chopped apples
¾ cup raisins or currants
2 tablespoons honey
¼ cup chopped walnuts
1 tablespoon grated lemon zest
1 tablespoon grated orange zest
½ cup apple juice
1½ teaspoons ground cinnamon
½ teaspoon ground nutmeg
¼ teaspoon ground cloves
¼ teaspoon ground allspice
1 unbaked 9-inch pie shell

Combine all ingredients, except pie shell, in a saucepan. Bring to a boil over medium heat, then lower to simmer. Cook 30 minutes, or until thick. Stir occasionally to prevent sticking. Preheat the oven to 400°F. Pour cooked filling into pie shell. Bake for 20 to 25 minutes. Cool and cut into 8 slices to serve.

Makes 8 servings
One serving of 1 slice = 1 starch + 2 fruits + 1 fat

Nutritive Values Per Serving

Calories	Carbohydrates	Protein	Fat	Sodium	Potassium	Cholesterol
229	39 g	3 g	8 g	101 mg	257 mg	0 mg

Plum Pudding

¾ cup whole wheat flour
½ teaspoon ground cinnamon
¼ teaspoon ground nutmeg
½ teaspoon baking soda
¼ cup margarine or butter
¾ cup (about 2 slices) whole wheat
    bread crumbs
½ cup raisins
½ cup walnuts
1 teaspoon grated orange zest
½ teaspoon grated lemon zest
1 egg
2 tablespoons honey
2 tablespoons molasses
⅓ cup skim milk

*P*reheat the oven to 350°F. Combine flour, cinnamon, nutmeg, and baking soda in a mixing bowl. Stir to blend. Cut in margarine or butter with a fork or pastry blender. Add the rest of the ingredients. Beat well. Pour batter into an oiled 1½-quart casserole dish fitted with waxed paper for easy removal. Bake for 50 to 60 minutes, or until a toothpick inserted into the center comes out clean. Cool for 10 minutes; lift from pan. Serve immediately or cool thoroughly before wrapping up for holiday sampling. Store in refrigerator. Reheat before serving. Cut into 8 slices.

Makes 8 servings
One serving = 1 starch + 1 fruit + 2 fats

Nutritive Values Per Serving

Calories	Carbohydrates	Protein	Fat	Sodium	Potassium	Cholesterol
225	29 g	4 g	11 g	194 mg	238 mg	23 mg

Christmas Stollen

½ cup dark or golden raisins
½ cup chopped dried apricots
¼ cup unsweetened apple juice or rum
1 package (or 1 tablespoon) active dry yeast
⅓ cup milk, heated to lukewarm (105° to 110°F)
½ cup all-purpose flour
½ cup margarine or butter
¼ cup sugar
¼ teaspoon salt
¼ teaspoon almond extract
1 teaspoon grated lemon zest
1 to 1½ cups all-purpose flour
½ cup sliced blanched almonds
½ cup low-sugar apricot preserves

Combine the raisins, apricots, and apple juice or rum in a bowl. Let soak overnight, or for at least 4 hours. Combine the yeast, milk, and ½ cup flour in a bowl. Mix until smooth and the mixture looks like thin mashed potatoes. Cover the bowl with a damp cloth and let rise in a warm place for 10 minutes, or until doubled in bulk.

Meanwhile, cream the margarine or butter, sugar, salt, almond extract, and lemon zest. Beat in the yeast mixture and 1¼ cups flour. Turn the dough out onto a lightly floured surface and knead in about ¼ cup more flour, enough flour to make the dough soft but not sticky. Knead for 3 minutes. Put in a greased bowl, cover with a damp towel, and let rise in a warm place until doubled, about 1½ to 2 hours.

Once the dough has doubled, knead in the raisin mixture and almonds. Knead until well mixed. Roll the dough into a rectangular 12″ × 6″ shape. Roll up jelly-roll fashion. Place on a lightly oiled baking sheet and let rise about 30 minutes.

Preheat the oven to 375°F and bake for 25 to 30 minutes, or until golden brown. Cool partially on a wire rack. Glaze the cool—but not cold—stollen with the apricot preserves. Cut into 15 equal slices.

Makes 15 servings
One serving of 1 slice = 1 starch + 1 fruit + 2 fats

Nutritive Values Per Serving

Calories	Carbohydrates	Protein	Fat	Sodium	Potassium	Cholesterol
197	27 g	3 g	9 g	159 mg	150 mg	1 mg

Fruit Cake

2 eggs
¼ cup honey
3 tablespoons vegetable oil
1 tablespoon brandy extract
1 teaspoon grated orange zest
1 cup all-purpose flour
¼ cup oatmeal
1 tablespoon baking powder
½ teaspoon ground allspice
1 8-ounce can unsweetened crushed
   pineapple, drained
½ cup raisins
1 cup candied fruit mix
½ cup chopped walnuts

*P*reheat the oven to 325°F. Cream together eggs, honey, oil, brandy extract, and orange zest. Add the rest of the ingredients and mix well. Pour batter into an oiled and floured 9″ × 5″ loaf pan. Bake for 50 to 60 minutes, or until center of cake springs back when pressed. Cool in the pan for 30 to 40 minutes. Remove from the pan; cool thoroughly. Wrap and store until ready to serve.

Makes 12 servings
One serving of 1 slice = 1 starch + 1 fruit + 1 fat

Nutritive Values Per Serving

Calories	Carbohydrates	Protein	Fat	Sodium	Potassium	Cholesterol
210	34 g	3 g	8 g	48 mg	141 mg	30 mg

Rolled Sugar Cookies

½ cup margarine or butter
¾ cup sugar
1 teaspoon vanilla extract
1 egg
2 cups all-purpose flour
1 tablespoon baking powder

Cream together the margarine or butter, sugar, vanilla, and egg until light and fluffy. Add the flour and baking powder. Blend until well mixed. Chill the dough for 2 hours, or overnight.

Preheat the oven to 375°F. Roll out dough on a lightly floured surface to ⅛ inch thick. Cut with a cookie cutter. Place on an ungreased baking sheet. Bake until lightly browned, about 10 minutes. Cool before storing.

Makes 72 cookies
One serving of 2 cookies = 1 starch

Nutritive Values Per Serving

Calories	Carbohydrates	Protein	Fat	Sodium	Potassium	Cholesterol
66	10 g	1 g	3 g	32 mg	10 mg	6 mg

Gingerbread Cutouts

½ cup margarine or butter
¼ cup sugar
½ cup molasses
1 egg
1 tablespoon vinegar
2½ to 3 cups all-purpose flour
2 teaspoons baking powder
½ teaspoon baking soda
1 teaspoon ground ginger
½ teaspoon ground cinnamon
¼ teaspoon ground cloves

*B*eat together margarine or butter, sugar, molasses, and egg. Add the rest of the ingredients, using 2½ cups flour. If batter is still very sticky, add ½ cup more flour and blend well. Cover dough and chill thoroughly, at least 3 hours, until dough is easier to handle.

Preheat the oven to 375°F. Divide chilled dough in half. Roll each half of dough onto a well-floured surface. Cut dough into desired shapes using cookie cutters. Place 1 inch apart on an oiled baking sheet. Bake for 5 to 10 minutes, or until edges are lightly browned. Cool thoroughly.

Makes 24 medium cookies
One serving of 1 cookie = 1 starch + 1 fat

Nutritive Values Per Serving

Calories	Carbohydrates	Protein	Fat	Sodium	Potassium	Cholesterol
119	19 g	2 g	4 g	49 mg	119 mg	8 mg

Brown Sugar Spritz Cookies

¾ cup margarine or butter
½ cup brown sugar, packed firm
1 egg
1 teaspoon grated lemon zest
½ teaspoon vanilla extract
¼ teaspoon almond extract
2⅔ cups all-purpose flour
1 teaspoon baking powder
Colored sugars

*P*reheat the oven to 375°F. Cream together margarine or butter, brown sugar, and egg. Add the rest of the ingredients, except colored sugars. Beat well. Mixture will be stiff. Spoon unchilled dough into a cookie press. Force dough through the cookie press onto an ungreased cookie sheet. Decorate with colored sugars. Bake for 7 to 10 minutes, or until edges are firm but not browned. Cool on a wire rack.

Makes 48 cookies
One serving of 2 cookies = 1 starch + 1 fat

Nutritive Values Per Serving

Calories	Carbohydrates	Protein	Fat	Sodium	Potassium	Cholesterol
116	4 g	2 g	6 g	70 mg	30 mg	8 mg

Hot Wassail

4 cups (1 quart) unsweetened apple juice
3 cups unsweetened pineapple juice
2 cups low-sugar cranberry juice cocktail
½ teaspoon ground nutmeg
2 cinnamon sticks
6 whole cloves
6 to 8 lemon slices

Combine all ingredients in a large kettle and simmer for 10 minutes. Serve hot.

Makes 9 cups or 18 servings
One serving of ½ cup = 1 fruit

Nutritive Values Per Serving

Calories	Carbohydrates	Protein	Fat	Sodium	Potassium	Cholesterol
54	14 g	0 g	0 g	3 mg	127 mg	0 mg

Low-Calorie Eggnog

2 eggs, separated
4 cups skim milk
1 teaspoon vanilla extract
1 tablespoon sugar
½ teaspoon brandy or rum extract
Ground nutmeg

Combine egg yolks and milk in a saucepan. Cook over medium heat until the mixture coats a metal spoon. Cool. Beat the egg whites on high speed of an electric mixer until soft peaks form. Add beaten egg whites, vanilla, sugar, and brandy or rum extract to the egg custard mixture. Mix lightly. Cover and chill. Pour into serving cups and sprinkle with nutmeg.

Makes 4 cups or 8 servings
One serving of ½ cup = 1 low-fat milk

Nutritive Values Per Serving

Calories	Carbohydrates	Protein	Fat	Sodium	Potassium	Cholesterol
65	8 g	6 g	1 g	77 mg	216 mg	48 mg

8

Other Favorites

White Chocolate Soufflé

¼ cup margarine or butter
¼ cup all-purpose flour
1 cup skim milk
3 eggs, separated
¼ teaspoon almond extract
4 ounces white chocolate, grated

*P*reheat the oven to 350°F. Combine margarine or butter and flour in a saucepan. Cook over medium heat for 2 minutes, stirring constantly. Gradually stir in milk; cook until smooth and thick, about 3 minutes, stirring constantly. Remove from heat. Beat in egg yolks and almond extract. Beat egg whites at high speed of an electric mixer until stiff, but not dry. Gently fold egg whites and white chocolate into egg yolk mixture. Pour into an ungreased 1½-quart casserole or soufflé dish. Bake for about 35 to 45 minutes, until risen and set, when a knife inserted in the center comes out clean. Serve immediately by spooning onto plates and topping with Raspberry Sauce (see Index).

Makes 6 servings
One serving of 1 piece with sauce = 1 starch + 3 fats

Nutritive Values Per Serving

Calories	Carbohydrates	Protein	Fat	Sodium	Potassium	Cholesterol
234	18 g	6 g	16 g	154 mg	161 mg	92 mg

Raspberry Sauce

1 cup white grape juice or apple juice
1 tablespoon sugar
1 tablespoon cornstarch
1 cup fresh raspberries

Combine grape or apple juice, sugar, and cornstarch in a saucepan. Cook over medium heat until thick and clear, stirring constantly. Remove from heat. Cool. Stir in raspberries. Serve warm over White Chocolate Soufflé (see Index).

Makes 1½ cups sauce
One serving of ½ cup = 1 fruit

Nutritive Values Per Serving

Calories	Carbohydrates	Protein	Fat	Sodium	Potassium	Cholesterol
43	11 g	0 g	0 g	1 mg	80 mg	0 mg

Amaretto Chocolate Mousse

2 ounces semisweet baking chocolate,
    chopped
½ cup evaporated skim milk
2 tablespoons sugar
2 egg yolks
1 tablespoon amaretto liqueur *or*
    ½ teaspoon almond extract
4 egg whites
Grated orange zest

Combine chocolate, milk, and sugar in a saucepan. Melt chocolate over medium heat, stirring constantly until smooth. Pour chocolate mixture into a bowl. Stir in egg yolks and beat thoroughly. Stir in amaretto or almond extract. Cool. When chocolate mixture is cool, beat egg whites in another bowl at high speed of an electric mixer until soft peaks form. Drizzle chocolate mixture over egg whites. Gently fold chocolate mixture into egg whites. Spoon into 4 parfait dishes. Chill 2 to 3 hours or until firm. Top with orange zest before serving.

Makes 4 servings
One serving = 1 milk + 2 fats

Nutritive Values Per Serving

Calories	Carbohydrates	Protein	Fat	Sodium	Potassium	Cholesterol
159	16 g	7 g	9 g	71 mg	267 mg	109 mg

Pineapple Coconut Rice Pudding

1 cup brown rice
2 tablespoons currants or raisins
1½ cups water
½ teaspoon salt
8 ounces canned, crushed, unsweetened pineapple
2 tablespoons flaked coconut, toasted
1 cup (8 ounces) low-fat vanilla yogurt

*P*ut rice and currants into saucepan. Add water and salt. Heat to boiling over high heat. Reduce heat to simmer and cook until water is absorbed and rice is tender, about 40 minutes. Add pineapple. Let rice continue cooking for an additional 10 minutes. Spoon into 6 serving dishes. Top with coconut. Serve with vanilla yogurt on top.

Makes 6 servings
One serving = 1 starch + 2 fruit

Nutritive Values Per Serving

Calories	Carbohydrates	Protein	Fat	Sodium	Potassium	Cholesterol
190	39 g	5 g	2 g	228 mg	232 mg	2 mg

Date Pecan Custard

2 eggs
2 cups skim milk
3 tablespoons sugar
½ cup finely chopped dates
¼ cup chopped pecans
¼ teaspoon ground nutmeg

*P*reheat the oven to 325°F. Combine all ingredients in a mixing bowl. Beat well. Pour into a 1½-quart baking dish that has been lightly oiled on the bottom and sides. Set the baking dish in a pan of hot water, about 1 inch deep. Bake for 40 to 45 minutes, or until a knife inserted into the center comes out clean. Spoon into 6 serving dishes.

Makes 6 servings
One serving = 1 low-fat milk + 1 fruit

Nutritive Values Per Serving

Calories	Carbohydrates	Protein	Fat	Sodium	Potassium	Cholesterol
145	21 g	5 g	5 g	61 mg	264 mg	63 mg

Lemony Bread Pudding

4 slices whole wheat bread
1 package (3.4 ounces) sugar-free
    instant vanilla pudding mix
1½ cups skim milk
½ cup (4 ounces) lemon yogurt
Ground nutmeg

*P*reheat the oven to 350°F. Cut bread into cubes and place in a lightly oiled 1-quart baking dish. Combine vanilla pudding, skim milk, and yogurt in a mixing bowl. Stir to blend. Pour over bread cubes. Sprinkle nutmeg over top. Bake for 20 to 30 minutes, or until a knife inserted into the center comes out clean.

Makes 4 servings
One serving = 1 starch + 1 low-fat milk

Nutritive Values Per Serving

Calories	Carbohydrates	Protein	Fat	Sodium	Potassium	Cholesterol
183	29 g	7 g	1.5 g	361 mg	217 mg	4 mg

Blueberry Kamut Ambrosia

1 cup kamut or wheat berries
    (or brown rice, cooked according to
    package directions)
1 teaspoon fresh grated ginger
½ teaspoon grated lemon zest
⅛ teaspoon ground allspice
¼ teaspoon ground cinnamon
⅛ teaspoon ground cloves
½ cup (4 ounces) nonfat vanilla yogurt
1 teaspoon honey
1 cup fresh blueberries or strawberries
¼ cup coconut

Place kamut in a bowl and cover with water. Let soak overnight. Drain off water. Put kernels into saucepan and add enough water to cover. Bring to a boil; reduce heat and cover. Cook 30 minutes, or until tender. Pour kamut into a mixing bowl and refrigerate. Combine the rest of the ingredients. Stir into chilled kamut. Toss gently to mix. Serve chilled.

Makes 4 servings
One serving = 2 starches + 1 fruit + 1 fat

Nutritive Values Per Serving

Calories	Carbohydrates	Protein	Fat	Sodium	Potassium	Cholesterol
260	52 g	6 g	4 g	42 mg	223 mg	1 mg

Cheese Crepes with Fruit Sauce

Crepes
1 cup flour
½ teaspoon baking powder
¼ teaspoon salt
2 eggs
1 cup skim milk
1 tablespoon margarine or butter

Cheese Filling
1 cup low-fat cottage cheese
¼ teaspoon ground cinnamon
¼ teaspoon grated orange zest

Fruit Sauce
¾ cup orange juice
1 tablespoon cornstarch
1 cup fresh or frozen fruit pieces
    (peaches, blueberries, strawberries)

Blend flour, baking powder, salt, eggs, and milk to make crepe batter. Melt a small amount of margarine or butter in a skillet and pour in a small amount of batter. Swirl batter around pan to form a thin crepe. When edges are lightly browned and cooked, remove crepe from skillet and continue with the rest of the batter.

To make the cheese filling, puree cottage cheese in a food processor or blender. Add cinnamon and orange zest. Put 2 tablespoons cheese mixture on each crepe and roll up. Place rolled crepes into a chafing dish and heat 10 to 15 minutes.

Make sauce by combining orange juice and cornstarch. Heat over medium heat until mixture thickens. Add fruit and boil 1 minute. Serve warm over crepes.

One serving of 2 crepes with sauce =
1 starch + 1 medium-fat protein

Nutritive Values Per Serving

Calories	Carbohydrates	Protein	Fat	Sodium	Potassium	Cholesterol
150	20 g	10 g	4 g	234 mg	194 mg	66 mg

Crepe Gâteau

2 eggs
½ cup all-purpose flour
1 tablespoon sugar
½ cup low-fat milk
1 tablespoon margarine or butter, melted
Powdered sugar

Combine all ingredients, except powdered sugar, in a food processor or blender. Mix to blend. Pour batter into a hot, lightly oiled crepe pan or non-stick skillet. When crepe is dry around the edges, turn over to brown. Repeat with remaining batter to make 8 crepes. Cool each crepe before filling. Spoon on a filling (Yogurt Cheese [see Index] or custard used in Cream Puffs [see Index]) and roll up. Place each roll on a serving plate. Top with a light sprinkling of powdered sugar just before serving.

Makes 8 servings
One serving of 1 crepe with filling = 1 starch + 1 fat

Nutritive Values Per Serving

Calories	Carbohydrates	Protein	Fat	Sodium	Potassium	Cholesterol
92	18 g	6 g	6 g	67 mg	79 mg	71 mg

Yogurt Cheese

1 cup (8 ounces) nonfat vanilla yogurt

*P*lace yogurt in a coffee filter inside a colander or strainer. Let stand at room temperature overnight to drain off liquid. What remains in the filter is the yogurt cheese.

Makes ½ cup yogurt cheese
One serving of 1 tablespoon = Free

Nutritive Values Per Serving

Calories	Carbohydrates	Protein	Fat	Sodium	Potassium	Cholesterol
26	5 g	1 g	0 g	20 mg	62 mg	1 mg

Banana Slices in Rhubarb Sauce

6 cups fresh or frozen rhubarb, cut into pieces
¼ cup orange juice
½ cup sugar
1 tablespoon grated orange zest
1 teaspoon ground cinnamon
3 medium bananas
¼ cup toasted slivered almonds

Combine rhubarb, orange juice, sugar, orange zest, and cinnamon in a saucepan. Bring to a boil, simmer for 10 minutes or until rhubarb begins to fall apart. Chill. At serving time, slice bananas into dessert dishes. Top with rhubarb sauce. Sprinkle with nuts.

Makes 6 servings
One serving = 1 starch + 1 fruit + 1 fat

Nutritive Values Per Serving

Calories	Carbohydrates	Protein	Fat	Sodium	Potassium	Cholesterol
189	38 g	3 g	4 g	57 mg	650 mg	0 mg

Pears and Berries Soup

3 peeled and cored pears, chopped
½ cup fresh or frozen raspberries
½ teaspoon ground cinnamon
1½ cups low-calorie cranberry juice cocktail
Nonfat vanilla yogurt

*P*uree pears and raspberries in a food processor or blender, along with cinnamon and cranberry juice cocktail. Chill. When ready to serve, pour into serving dishes and garnish with a dollop of yogurt.

Makes 6 cups or 6 servings
One serving of 1 cup = 1 fruit

Nutritive Values Per Serving

Calories	Carbohydrates	Protein	Fat	Sodium	Potassium	Cholesterol
81	19 g	1 g	0 g	14 mg	173 mg	1 mg

Chilled Melon Soup

1 honeydew melon, seeded and
    cut into small cubes
¼ cup white grape juice
1 tablespoon honey
Juice of 2 limes (4 tablespoons)
Sliced fresh strawberries

Combine melon and grape juice in a food processor or blender with honey and lime juice. Puree until smooth. Chill until ready to serve. Pour into dessert bowls or champagne glasses. Garnish with strawberry slices.

Makes 5 cups or 6 servings
One serving of about ⅘ cup = 2 fruits

Nutritive Values Per Serving

Calories	Carbohydrates	Protein	Fat	Sodium	Potassium	Cholesterol
99	26 g	1 g	0 g	22 mg	630 mg	0 mg

Brandied Fruits

1 pint strawberries
1 cup raspberries
1 cup blueberries
4 teaspoons brandy extract
1 tablespoon sugar

Combine fruit in a covered dish or large glass jar with a tight-fitting lid. Add brandy extract and sugar. Stir gently to mix. Refrigerate 2 days before serving.

Makes 4 cups or 4 servings
One serving of 1 cup = 1 fruit

Nutritive Values Per Serving

Calories	Carbohydrates	Protein	Fat	Sodium	Potassium	Cholesterol
70	17 g	1 g	0 g	2 mg	202 mg	0 mg

Peanutty Popcorn Snack

1 cup peanut butter
¼ cup honey
8 cups popped corn

*H*eat peanut butter and honey until blended. Pour over popped corn and toss to coat. Cool before serving.

Makes 8 cups or 8 servings
One serving of 1 cup =
1 starch + 1 medium-fat protein + 1 fat

Nutritive Values Per Serving

Calories	Carbohydrates	Protein	Fat	Sodium	Potassium	Cholesterol
158	8 g	6 g	9 g	80 mg	140 mg	0 mg

9

Dessert Beverages

Peach Smoothie

---

2 peaches, peeled and seeded
1 cup (8 ounces) low-fat vanilla yogurt
2 teaspoons lemon juice
1 teaspoon rum extract

Combine all ingredients in a food processor or blender. Process until smooth. Pour over crushed ice in 4 champagne glasses.

Makes 4 servings
One serving = 1 fruit

Nutritive Values Per Serving

Calories	Carbohydrates	Protein	Fat	Sodium	Potassium	Cholesterol
58	10 g	3 g	1 g	37 mg	169 mg	3 mg

Banana Tofu Nog

½ cup skim milk
1 ripe banana
1 tablespoon honey
½ package (4 ounces) firm tofu *or*
    1 cup plain yogurt
Ground nutmeg

Combine milk, banana, honey, and tofu in a food proces-sor or blender. Process until smooth. Pour over crushed ice in 4 champagne glasses. Sprinkle surface with nutmeg.

Makes 4 servings
One serving = 1 low-fat milk

Nutritive Values Per Serving

Calories	Carbohydrates	Protein	Fat	Sodium	Potassium	Cholesterol
100	14 g	6 g	3 g	21 mg	245 mg	1 mg

Orange Cider

3 ounces frozen orange juice concentrate,
    thawed
1½ cups water
1 cup apple cider or apple juice
6 cloves
1 2-inch piece stick cinnamon
Orange slices

Combine orange juice concentrate, water, apple cider, cloves, and cinnamon in a saucepan. Simmer for 10 minutes to blend flavors. Serve warm. Garnish with orange slices.

Makes 6 servings
One serving of ½ cup = 1 fruit

Nutritive Values Per Serving

Calories	Carbohydrates	Protein	Fat	Sodium	Potassium	Cholesterol
43	11 g	0 g	0 g	2 mg	182 mg	0 mg

Hot Cranberry Grog

4 cups low-calorie cranberry juice cocktail
½ cup pineapple juice
¼ teaspoon ground allspice
6 whole cloves
Dash ground nutmeg

Combine all ingredients in saucepan. Bring to a boil. Remove from heat and let stand 15 minutes to blend flavors. Serve immediately.

Makes 5 servings
One serving of about ¾ cup = 1 fruit

Nutritive Values Per Serving

Calories	Carbohydrates	Protein	Fat	Sodium	Potassium	Cholesterol
50	12 g	0 g	0 g	6 mg	75 mg	0 mg

Cranberry Punch

4 cups low-sugar cranberry juice cocktail
2 cups orange juice
12 ounces sugar-free lemon-lime
    carbonated beverage
1 teaspoon ground cardamom
Whole cranberries
Holly leaves

Combine the cranberry and orange juices in a punch bowl.
Pour the carbonated beverage down the sides of the bowl.
Sprinkle on cardamom. Float whole cranberries and holly
leaves on top.

Makes 8 cups or 16 servings
One serving of ½ cup = ½ fruit

Nutritive Values Per Serving

Calories	Carbohydrates	Protein	Fat	Sodium	Potassium	Cholesterol
25	6 g	0 g	0 g	2 mg	72 mg	0 mg

Appendix:
Exchange Lists for
Meal Planning

*E*xchange lists are foods listed together because they are similar in carbohydrate, protein, and fat content. Each food has a serving size indicated. The reason for this food grouping is to allow an exchange of similar foods within the same list. An example is trading a slice of bread for ½ cup oatmeal in a breakfast menu.

The exchange list system of meal planning provides a lot of food choices and allows good variety in menus. Foods listed in the same exchange list provide similar amounts of nutrients per serving.

These food exchange lists are produced by the American Diabetes Association and the American Dietetic Association as part of a series of nutritional education resources for people with diabetes. Some of the foods listed in *Exchange Lists for Meal Planning* are provided for quick reference in modifying your meal plan. The lists are based on the most current nutrient data available.

Starch List

Each food in this list contains about 15 grams of carbohydrate, 3 grams of protein, 1 gram or less of fat, and about 80 calories per serving. In general one starch exchange is:

- ½ cup cereal, pasta, or starchy vegetable
- 1 ounce of a bread product or 1 slice of bread
- ¾ to 1 ounce of most snack foods (some snack foods may have extra fat)

Breads

Bagel .... ½ (1 ounce)

Bread, reduced calorie .... 2 slices (1½ ounces)

Bread (white, whole wheat, pumpernickel, or rye) .... 1 slice (1 ounce)

Bread sticks, crisp, 4 inches long by ½ inch .... 2 (⅔ ounce)

English muffin .... ½

Hog dog or hamburger bun .... ½ (1 ounce)

Pita, 6 inches across .... ½

Roll, plain, small .... 1 (1 ounce)

Raisin bread, unfrosted ....1 slice (1 ounce)
Tortilla, corn, 6 inches across..........................1
Tortilla, flour, 7–8 inches across 1
Waffle, 4½-inch square, reduced-fat 1

Cereals and Grains

Bran cereals...½ cup
Bulgur..½ cup
Cereals, cooked ....½ cup
Cereals, unsweetened, ready-to-eat ....¾ cup
Cornmeal, dry..................................3 tablespoons
Couscous...⅓ cup
Flour, dry ....3 tablespoons
Granola, low-fat...¼ cup
Grape Nuts ....¼ cup
Grits...½ cup
Kasha ....½ cup

Millet .... ¼ cup
Muesli .... ¼ cup
Oats .... ½ cup
Pasta .... ½ cup
Puffed cereal .... 1½ cups
Rice milk .... ½ cup
Rice, white or brown .... ⅓ cup
Shredded Wheat .... ½ cup
Sugar-frosted cereal .... ½ cup
Wheat germ .... 3 tablespoons

Starchy Vegetables

Baked beans .... ⅓ cup
Corn .... ½ cup
Corn on the cob, medium .... 1 (5 ounces)
Mixed vegetables with corn, peas, or pasta .... 1 cup
Peas, green .... ½ cup

Plantain .... ½ cup
Potato, baked or boiled .... 1 small (3 ounces)
Potato, mashed .... ½ cup
Squash, winter (acorn or butternut) ..... 1 cup
Yam or sweet potato, plain .... ½ cup

Crackers and Snacks

Animal crackers 8
Graham crackers, 2½-inch square 3
Matzo .... ¾ ounce
Melba toast .... 4 slices
Oyster crackers 24
Popcorn (popped, no-fat-added or low-fat microwave) ..... 3 cups
Pretzels .... ¾ ounce
Rice cakes, 4 inches across 2
Saltine-type crackers 6
Snack chips, fat-free (tortilla or potato) ..... 15–20 (¾ ounce)
Whole wheat crackers, no-fat-added ..... 2–5 (¾ ounce)

Starchy Foods Prepared with Fat

(count as 1 starch exchange + 1 fat exchange)

Biscuit, 2½ inches across 1

Chow mein noodles .... ½ cup

Cornbread, 2-inch cube .... 1 (2 ounces)

Crackers, round butter-type 6

Croutons .... 1 cup

French fried potatoes .... 16–25 (3 ounces)

Granola .... ¼ cup

Muffin, small .... 1 (1½ ounces)

Pancake, 4 inches across 2

Popcorn, microwave, fat added .... 3 cups

Sandwich crackers, cheese or peanut butter filling 3

Stuffing, bread (prepared) .... ⅓ cup

Taco shell, 6 inches across 2

Waffle, 4½-inch square 1

Whole wheat crackers, fat added .... 4–6 (1 ounce)

Fruit List

Each food in this list contains about 15 grams of carbohydrate and 60 calories per serving. In general one fruit exchange is:

- 1 small to medium fresh fruit
- ½ cup canned or fresh fruit or fruit juice
- ¼ cup dried fruit

Fruit

Apple, unpeeled, small ....1 (4 ounces)
Applesauce, unsweetened ....½ cup
Apples, dried ....4 rings
Apricots, fresh ....4 whole (5½ ounces)
Apricots, dried ....8 halves
Apricots, canned...½ cup
Banana, small ....1 (4 ounces)
Blackberries...¾ cup

Blueberries ....¾ cup

Cantaloupe, small ....⅓ melon (11 ounces) or 1 cup cubes

Cherries, sweet, fresh..12 (3 ounces)

Cherries, sweet, canned...½ cup

Dates 3

Figs, fresh ....1½ large or 2 medium (3½ ounces)

Figs, dried 1½

Fruit cocktail..½ cup

Grapefruit, large..½ (11 ounces)

Grapefruit sections, canned ....¾ cup

Grapes, small ....17 (3 ounces)

Honeydew melon ....1 slice (10 ounces) or 1 cup cubes

Kiwi..1 (3½ ounces)

Mandarin oranges, canned..¾ cup

Mango, small ....½ fruit (5½ ounces) or ½ cup

Nectarine, small..1 (5 ounces)

Orange, small ....1 (6½ ounces)

Papaya ....½ fruit (8 ounces) or 1 cup cubes
Peach, medium, fresh............1 (6 ounces)
Peaches, canned ....½ cup
Pear, large, fresh ....½ (4 ounces)
Pears, canned............½ cup
Pineapple, fresh ....¾ cup
Pineapple, canned............½ cup
Plums, small............2 (5 ounces)
Plums, canned ....½ cup
Prunes, dried 3
Raisins............2 tablespoons
Raspberries............1 cup
Strawberries............1¼ cups whole berries
Tangerines, small............2 (8 ounces)
Watermelon............1 slice (13½ ounces) or 1¼ cups cubes

Fruit Juice

Apple juice or cider .... ½ cup
Cranberry juice cocktail .... ⅓ cup
Cranberry juice cocktail, reduced-calorie .... 1 cup
Fruit juice blends, 100% juice .... ⅓ cup
Grape juice .... ⅓ cup
Grapefruit juice .... ½ cup
Orange juice .... ½ cup
Pineapple juice .... ½ cup
Prune juice .... ⅓ cup

Milk List

Each serving of milk or milk product in this list contains about 12 grams of carbohydrate and 8 grams of protein. The amount of fat in the milk (0 to 8 grams per serving) determines whether it is identified as skim/very low-fat milk, low-fat milk, or whole milk. In general one milk exchange is 1 cup.

Skim and Very Low-Fat Milk
(0–3 grams of fat per serving)

Skim milk...1 cup
½% milk..1 cup
1% milk...1 cup
Nonfat or low-fat buttermilk ....1 cup
Evaporated skim milk ....½ cup
Nonfat dry milk..⅓ cup (dry)
Plain nonfat yogurt.......................................¾ cup
Nonfat or low-fat fruit-flavored yogurt sweetened with aspartame or a non-nutritive sweetener...1 cup

Low-Fat Milk
(5 grams of fat per serving)

2% milk .... 1 cup
Plain low-fat yogurt .... 3/4 cup
Sweet acidophilus milk .... 1 cup

Whole Milk
(8 grams of fat per serving)

Whole milk .... 1 cup
Evaporated whole milk .... 1/2 cup
Goat's milk .... 1 cup
Kefir .... 1 cup

Other Carbohydrates

This group of foods allows for substitution of any food choice on the list for a starch, a fruit, or a milk in your daily meal plan. These foods can be substituted even though they contain added sugars or fat. Because many of these foods are concentrated sources of carbohydrate and fat, the portion sizes are usually small.

Food	Serving Size	Exchanges Per Serving
Angel food cake, unfrosted	1/12th cake	2 carbohydrates
Brownie, small, unfrosted	2-inch square	1 carbohydrate, 1 fat
Cake, unfrosted	2-inch square	1 carbohydrate, 1 fat
Cake, frosted	2-inch square	2 carbohydrates, 1 fat
Cookie, fat-free	2 small	1 carbohydrate
Cookie or sandwich cookie with creme filling	2 small	1 carbohydrate, 1 fat
Cupcake, frosted	1 small	2 carbohydrates, 1 fat
Cranberry sauce, jellied	1/4 cup	2 carbohydrates
Doughnut, plain cake	1 medium (1 1/2 ounces)	1 1/2 carbohydrates, 2 fats

Doughnut, glazed ....3¾ inches across (2 ounces) ....2 carbohydrates, 2 fats

Fruit juice bars, frozen, 100% juice ....1 bar (3 ounces) ....1 carbohydrate

Fruit snacks, chewy (pureed
    fruit concentrate) ....1 roll (¾ ounce) ....1 carbohydrate

Fruit spreads, 100% fruit ....1 tablespoon ....1 carbohydrate

Gelatin, regular...½ cup..1 carbohydrate

Gingersnaps..3...1 carbohydrate

Granola bar ....1 bar ....1 carbohydrate, 1 fat

Granola bar, fat-free....................................1 bar ....2 carbohydrates

Hummus..⅓ cup ....1 carbohydrate, 1 fat

Ice cream ....½ cup..1 carbohydrate, 2 fats

Ice cream, light..½ cup..1 carbohydrate, 1 fat

Ice cream, fat-free, no-sugar-added............½ cup...1 carbohydrate

Jam or jelly, regular....................................1 tablespoon ....1 carbohydrate

Milk, chocolate, whole ....1 cup ....2 carbohydrates, 1 fat

Pie, fruit, two crusts....................................⅙ pie..3 carbohydrates, 2 fats

Pie, pumpkin or custard..............................⅛ pie ....1 carbohydrate, 2 fats

Food	Serving Size	Exchanges Per Serving
Potato chips	12–18 (1 ounce)	1 carbohydrate, 2 fats
Pudding, regular		
(made with low-fat milk)	½ cup	2 carbohydrates
Pudding, sugar-free		
(made with low-fat milk)	½ cup	1 carbohydrate
Salad dressing, fat-free	¼ cup	1 carbohydrate
Sherbet, sorbet	½ cup	2 carbohydrates
Spaghetti or pasta sauce, canned	½ cup	1 carbohydrate, 1 fat
Sweet roll or Danish	1 (2½ ounces)	2½ carbohydrates, 2 fats
Syrup, light	2 tablespoons	1 carbohydrate
Syrup, regular	1 tablespoon	1 carbohydrate
Tortilla chips	6–12 (1 ounce)	1 carbohydrate, 2 fats
Yogurt, frozen, low-fat, fat-free	⅓ cup	1 carbohydrate, 0–1 fat
Yogurt, frozen, fat-free, no-sugar-added	½ cup	1 carbohydrate
Yogurt, low-fat with fruit	1 cup	3 carbohydrates, 0–1 fat
Vanilla wafers	5	1 carbohydrate, 1 fat

Index

Amaretto Chocolate Mousse,
107
Ambrosia, Blueberry Kamut,
111
Angel Food Cake, Deviled,
48; Fruit Sauce for, 49
Apple
and Cheese Pie, 59
Chocolate Delight, 64
Cobbler, 71
Applesauce Cake, 32
Apricot Oatmeal Squares, 20

Banana
Bread, 80
Dream Cake, 55
Slices in Rhubarb Sauce,
116
Tofu Nog, 124
Bar Cookies, 19–25. *See also*
Cookies
Apricot Oatmeal Squares,
20
Fudge Brownies, 24
Lemon Bars, 22
Peppermint Brownies, 25
Pineapple Cashew
Brownies, 23
Strawberry Tea Bars, 19
Berries and Pears Soup, 117
Beverage, 123–27
Banana Tofu Nog, 124
Cranberry Grog, Hot, 126
Cranberry Punch, 127

Eggnog, Low-Calorie, 101
Orange Cider, 125
Peach Smoothie, 123
Wassail, Hot, 100
Biscotti Nut Cookies, 14
blood glucose management, 3
Blueberry Kamut Ambrosia,
111
Brandied Fruits, 119
Bread(s). *See also* Muffins;
Quick Bread; Yeast
Bread
exchange lists (for meal
planning), 131–32
Pudding, Lemony, 110
Brioche, Chocolate Swirl, 86
Brown Sugar Spritz Cookies,
99
Brownies
Fudge, 24
Peppermint, 25
Pineapple Cashew, 23

Cake, 29–55. *See also* Quick
Bread; Yeast Bread
about exchange lists (for
meal planning), 142
Applesauce, 32
Banana Dream, 55
Cappuccino Pudding, 37
Caribbean Coconut
Mousse, 42
Carrot, 40
Chocolate Raisin, 41

Cookies and Cream
    Cheesecake, 30
Deviled Angel Food, 48;
    Fruit Sauce for, 49
Fruit, 96
Killer Chocolate, 52;
    White Chocolate Icing
    for, 54
No-Bake Hazelnut
    Graham, 29
Orange Fig, 34
Orange Torte, Fresh, 50;
    Creamy Orange Icing
    for, 51
Peachy Upside-Down, 44
Pineapple Upside-Down, 46
Poppy Seed Pound, 36
Pumpkin Cheesecake, 83
Sour Cream Coffee, 78
Southern Pecan Oatmeal,
    38
Stollen, Christmas, 94
calories and fat, 4
Cappuccino Pudding Cake, 37
carbohydrate intake, total, 3
carbohydrates (cakes pies,
    yogurt, etc.), exchange
    lists (for meal planning),
    142–44
Caribbean Coconut Mousse
    Cake, 42
Carrot Cake, 40
cereals, exchange lists (for
    meal planning), 132–33
Cheese
  and Apple Pie, 59
  Crepes with Fruit Sauce,
    112
  Yogurt, 115

Cheesecake, Cookies and
    Cream, 30
Cheesecake, Pumpkin, 83
Chocolate. See also White
    Chocolate
  Amaretto Mousse, 107
  Apple Delight, 64
  Cake, Killer, 52
  Chip Cookies, 8
  Cinnamon Crescent, 88
  Deviled Angel Food Cake,
    48
  Fudge Brownies, 24
  Peppermint Brownies, 25
  Raisin Cake, 41
  Swirl Brioche, 86
  Wafers, 13
Christmas Stollen, 94
Cider, Orange, 125
Coconut Mousse Cake,
    Caribbean, 42
Cookies, 7–16. See also Bar
    Cookies
  about exchange lists (for
    meal planning), 142
  Biscotti Nut, 14
  Brown Sugar Spritz, 99
  Chocolate Chip, 8
  Chocolate Wafers, 13
  and Cream Cheesecake, 30
  Gingerbread Cutouts, 98
  Gingersnaps, 10
  Hazelnut, 11
  Macadamia White
    Chocolate, 7
  Marsala Macaroons, 9
  Peanut Butter, 16
  Pumpkin Spice, 12
  Sugar, Rolled, 97

crackers and snacks, exchange lists (for meal planning), 134

Cranberry Grog, Hot, 126

Cranberry Punch, 127

Cream Puffs, 68

Crepe Gâteau, 114

Crepes, Cheese, with Fruit Sauce, 112

Custard, Date Pecan, 109

Date Pecan Custard, 109

Date Pumpkin Muffins, 77

Dessert. *See also* Cake; Pie; Quick Bread; Yeast Bread

about, 3–4

Amaretto Chocolate Mousse, 107

Banana Slices in Rhubarb Sauce, 116

Blueberry Kamut Ambrosia, 111

Brandied Fruits, 119

Cheese Crepes with Fruit Sauce, 112

Crepe Gâteau, 114

Date Pecan Custard, 109

Lemony Bread Pudding, 110

Melon Soup, Chilled, 118

Pears and Berries Soup, 117

Pineapple Coconut Rice Pudding, 108

Plum Pudding, 92

White Chocolate Soufflé, 105

Deviled Angel Food Cake, 48; Fruit Sauce for, 49

Drink. *See* Beverage

Eggnog, Low-Calorie, 101

exchange lists, 131–44. *See also* individual foods

Fig Orange Cake, 34

Fruit(s)

about exchange lists (for meal planning), 136–38

Brandied, 119

Cake, 96

juice, exchange lists (for meal planning), 139

Sauce (for Angel Food Cake), 49

Tart, 70

Fudge Brownies, 24

Gingerbread Cutouts, 98

Gingerbread Muffins, 75

Gingersnaps, 10

glycemic index, 3

grains, exchange lists (for meal planning), 132–33

Grog, Cranberry, Hot, 126

Hazelnut Cookies, 11

Hazelnut Graham Cake, No-Bake, 29

Holiday Favorites, 83–101. *See also* Cake; Cookies; Yeast Bread; etc.

ice cream, exchange lists (for meal planning), 143

Icing, Creamy Orange, 51
Icing, White Chocolate, 54

Key Lime Pie, 60
Killer Chocolate Cake, 52

Lemon Bars, 22
Lemony Bread Pudding, 110
Lime Pie, Key, 60
Low-Calorie Eggnog, 101

Macadamia White Chocolate
    Cookies, 7
Macaroons, Marsala, 9
Marsala Macaroons, 9
meal planning, exchange lists
    for, 131–44. *See also*
    individual foods
Melon Soup, Chilled, 118
milk, exchange lists (for meal
    planning), 140–41
Mincemeat Pie, 91
Mousse, Amaretto Chocolate,
    107
Mud Pie, 66
Muffins, 75–77
    Gingerbread, 75
    Pumpkin Date, 77
    Rhubarb Walnut, 76

No-Bake Hazelnut Graham
    Cake, 29

Oatmeal Apricot Squares, 20
Orange
    Cider, 125
    Fig Cake, 34
    Icing, Creamy, 51
    Torte, Fresh, 50

Pastry, 62–71
    Apple Cobbler, 71
    Chocolate Apple Delight,
        64
    Cream Puffs, 68
    Poppy Seed Crumble, 62
    Rhubarb Crumble, 67
Peach Smoothie, 123
Peachy Upside-Down Cake,
    44
Peanut Butter Cookies, 16
Peanutty Popcorn Snack, 120
Pears and Berries Soup, 117
Pecan
    Date Custard, 109
    Oatmeal Cake, Southern,
        38
    Tea Crescent, 84
Peppermint Brownies, 25
Pie, 59–60, 66, 70. *See also*
    Pastry
    about exchange lists (for
        meal planning), 143
    Apple and Cheese, 59
    Fruit Tart, 70
    Key Lime, 60
    Mincemeat, 91
    Mud, 66
    Pumpkin, 90
Pineapple
    Cashew Brownies, 23
    Coconut Rice Pudding,
        108
    Upside-Down Cake, 46
Plum Pudding, 92
Popcorn Snack, Peanutty,
    120
Poppy Seed Crumble, 62
Poppy Seed Pound Cake, 36

Pudding
  Bread, Lemony, 110
  Plum, 92
  Rice, Pineapple Coconut, 108
Pumpkin
  Cheesecake, 83
  Date Muffins, 77
  Pie, 90
  Raisin Bread, 79
  Spice Cookies, 12
Punch, Cranberry, 127

Quick Bread. *See also* Muffins; Yeast Bread
  Banana, 80
  Pumpkin Raisin, 79
  Sour Cream Coffee Cake, 78

Raisin Chocolate Cake, 41
Raisin Pumpkin Bread, 79
Raspberry Sauce, 106
Rhubarb
  Crumble, 67
  Sauce, Banana Slices in, 116
  Walnut Muffins, 76
Rice Pudding, Pineapple Coconut, 108

Sauce, Fruit, 49
Sauce, Raspberry, 106
Smoothie, Peach, 123
Soufflé, White Chocolate, 105
Soup. *See* Dessert
Sour Cream Coffee Cake, 78

Southern Pecan Oatmeal Cake, 38
Spritz Cookies, Brown Sugar, 99
starchy foods with fat, exchange lists (for meal planning), 135; starchy vegetables, 133–34
Stollen, Christmas, 94
Strawberry Tea Bars, 19
Sugar Cookies, Rolled, 97
sugar in the diet, 3

Upside-Down Cake, Peachy, 44
Upside-Down Cake, Pineapple, 46

vegetables, starchy, exchange lists (for meal planning), 133–34

Walnut Rhubarb Muffins, 76
Wassail, Hot, 100
White Chocolate
  Icing, 54
  Macadamia Cookies, 7
  Soufflé, 105; Raspberry Sauce for, 106

Yeast Bread
  Chocolate Cinnamon Crescent, 88
  Chocolate Swirl Brioche, 86
  Pecan Tea Crescent, 84
Yogurt Cheese, 115